Other WildBlue Press Books By Steve Jackson

Bogeyman: *He Was Every Parent's Nightmare*
http://wbp.bz/bogeyman

No Stone Unturned: *The True Story of the World's Premier Forensic Investigators*
http://wbp.bz/nsu

Rough Trade: *A Shocking True Story of Prostitution, Murder and Redemption*
http://wbp.bz/rt

STEVE JACKSON

SMOOTH TALKER TRAIL OF DEATH

STEVE JACKSON

NEW YORK TIMES BEST SELLING AUTHOR

WILDBLUE
PRESS

WildBluePress.com

Some names have been-changed to protect the privacy of individuals connected to this story.

NecroSearch International is a non-profit and tax-deductible donations and public inquiries can be made by writing: NecroSearch International, 1713 Willox Court, STE A, Fort Collins, CO 80524.

SMOOTH TALKER published by:
WILDBLUE PRESS
P.O. Box 102440
Denver, Colorado 80250

WILDBLUE PRESS is registered at the U.S. Patent and Trademark Offices.
ISBN 978-1-942266-43-3 Trade Paperback

ISBN 978-1-942266-44-0 eBook

Interior Formatting/Book Cover Design by Elijah Toten
www.totencreative.com

SMOOTH TALKER

STEVE JACKSON

PREFACE

He's just a fat old man rotting away in a Colorado prison.

Terrified that he's going to spend what's left of his life behind concrete walls, steel bars and concertina razor wire, he spends his days filing appeals and writs in a never-ending stream of bullshit and lies. But he'll die in prison. If not that one, then another, or another; they're lined up like graves in a cemetery waiting for him. And there'd probably be others if someone wanted to go through the effort of making him pay for all the death, despair and ruined lives he's caused. Just an evil old monster waiting for final justice.

But back in the day he'd been a charmer with his blue eyes and that soft south-Texas drawl. Not particularly handsome and already losing his hair by his thirties, but boy could he spin a tale. The Good Samaritan who'd offer to help with a flat tire, or clear some brush, or fix an appliance. Or just tell a good yarn about the places he'd been, the things he'd done. A smooth-talking son of bitch ... a real lady killer.

STEVE JACKSON

I

July 10, 1974

On a summer evening when the Napa Valley was baking like a brick oven, Anita Andrews parked her tan 1967 Cadillac in front of the old three-story building that housed the bar she and her sister had inherited from their father five years earlier. She then unlocked the padlock and turned on the red-and-white neon sign that hung above the front doors, the signal to her patrons that tonight *Fagiani's Cocktail Lounge* was open for business.

Not that she was happy to be there. A former county fair beauty queen, the 51-year-old Andrews didn't like working at the bar. She already had a full-time job as a secretary at the Napa State Hospital, a psychiatric facility that included housing for the criminally insane. But long hours there weren't the reason she dreaded going to *Fagiani's* as her second job.

Although she'd practically been raised in the bar and had many fond memories of her father from the place, she'd told friends that she hated going there now. It was in a bad area of town and not a nice place to hangout anymore, at least not for a woman. That stretch of Main Street near the Napa River was a motley collection of dives mostly serving the same barflies, assorted drifters, and outpatients from the psych ward who lived in the seedy Connor Hotel opposite the bar.

Such was Andrews' distaste for *Fagiani's* that she and her sister, Muriel Fagiani, opened the padlock and turned on the sign—complete with a bright white neon martini glass on top—only enough to maintain its liquor license, which stipulated they had to operate 24 hours a week. They intended to sell the lounge and the license would be needed to lure a prospective buyer. In the meantime, they did what they had to do. Muriel handled most of the finances, while Anita worked behind the bar pouring drinks, listening to hard luck stories, staying open until 9 or 11 p.m., and hoping for somebody to take it off their hands. They were still waiting on that hot night in July 1974.

Someday that neighborhood would change again, get nicer. But back then, Napa, and the valley from which it took its name, wasn't the pricey wine-tourist destination and playground for the wealthy from the Bay Area it would become in the next decade. With a population just shy of 34,000 souls, the town was still just a sleepy little county seat fifty miles north of San Francisco, surrounded by gently rolling hills and a bucolic patchwork of farms, pastures and the vineyards for which it had been known for more than a hundred years.

Once a jump off point for silver miners and known in the late-19th and early 20th centuries as having more bordellos than any other city its size in California, it was no great wonder that the town's first official business was a saloon on the corner of Third Street down by the river. Nichola Fagiani opened his lounge about a hundred years later.

A native of Italy, Fagiani had immigrated to the Napa Valley where he'd acquired a vineyard and winery. He'd sold that and purchased the old stone building on Main Street that had once housed a speakeasy during the Prohibition and opened his own place.

Back then "Papa's Bar," as his daughters' called it, was a nice place where a working man could bring his family for dinner, drinks and camaraderie. There was a pool table and a jukebox, and three deer heads on the wall overseeing everything. Nichola was the cook and head bartender while his daughters hung out and played with the kids of his customers.

Fagiani's bar where Anita Andrews was murdered July 10, 1974. Photo courtesy of the Napa County District Attorney's Office.

The family was staunchly Catholic and conservative; his daughters weren't allowed to wear pants, only dresses. They were both beautiful young women, which was acknowledged publicly when Anita was crowned queen of the Napa County Fair in 1940. *"I'm more than happy to have the honor, but a little sorry that Joan didn't win,"* the 17-year-old modestly told a reporter for the *Napa Valley Register*, referring to runner-up Joan Hofacre.

Anita graduated from Armstrong's Business School in Berkeley. Then two years later, in June 1942, she married Clarence "Mike" Andrews Jr. The couple moved to Berkeley and had two daughters, first Diana and then eight years later, Donna. However, the marriage didn't last and the couple divorced in 1951.

A few years later, Andrews moved with her daughters back to Napa. She was a single mother, which was unusual for those times, but she worked hard and emphasized the need to get a good education to her daughters.

Time passed, her daughters grew up and moved out and onto their own lives. She remained close to her father and the two often attended boxing matches and watched football together. When he died, she and Muriel, a former schoolteacher who moved back to Napa from Sacramento, inherited the bar. They had to work it themselves because it didn't bring in enough money to hire someone else.

Everybody in town knew Anita Andrews and her tan Cadillac. Neat and fastidious about her appearance, she always dressed well, wore a Bulova watch and, when she worked, a black diamond onyx ring so that those customers who didn't know her well would think she was married. As a secretary she always wore high heels, and then when she arrived at the bar, she'd change into flats; when she left for the night, she'd removed the flats and put the high heels back on.

Anita never remarried. There was an on-again, off-again boyfriend for awhile. No one seemed to know much about him other than he worked for a carnival and traveled a lot. But about a week earlier, she'd told her daughter, Debbie, that she was fed up with him. He'd run up a $400 phone bill at her apartment, and she was keeping his tools in the back of her car until he paid her back. But after that, she said, they were done.

Anita Andrews was 51 years old when she was killed. Photo courtesy of the Napa County District Attorney's Office.

Anita also had other long-time friends, like Joseph Silva, who'd lived next door to her on Main Street until he bought a home in 1973 and she moved to a new apartment on Soscol Avenue. He owned his own tan Cadillac, but his was a '52. They'd get together for coffee on some mornings, or just sit on the front porch chatting. She was outgoing and warm, and he enjoyed her company. They'd even made plans to go out to dinner the night before, but she called to ask for a rain check.

Andrews also told Silva she didn't like working at the bar. It scared her. One night she'd called him up and quietly said, *"I got some creep in here, would you call me back and pretend you're my boyfriend so I can get rid of him?"*[1]

Even the police looked out for Anita. There were no set hours for *Fagiani's,* but as part of his late night patrol down Main Street, the officer on duty would slow down as he passed the bar. If the padlock was off and the Cadillac parked out front, Fagiani's was open for business. If the Cadillac was gone, he'd shine his spotlight on the padlock to make sure the place was secured before driving on.

The evening of July 10 went like most nights at *Fagiani's.* Only a handful of people had stopped in. By late evening, the only customers were three local men who were carousing around town and drinking at one end of the bar counter, and another man sitting on a stool at the far end smoking cigarettes, cutting a pack of cards, and flirting with Andrews.

The three local men didn't recognize him, but he seemed to be a real smooth talker with a Southern drawl of some sort. He sat with his back to them and kept his face covered with his hand so they couldn't get a good look at him.

A little after 9 p.m., Andrews started cleaning up. She kept the place spotless and that included wiping the bar down until it shone, and lining all the stools up neatly beneath the counter, except where the stranger sat, his stool pushed out from the bar, smoking and drinking.

Finally, one of the three locals decided he didn't like the way the stranger kept hiding his face. "Hey, what's your problem?" he shouted.

However, Luce, who'd been in the bathroom when the commotion started, got his friend to stop badgering the other man. He then walked over and held out his hand. "We're not

---

1   *Anita E. Fagiani Andrews,* Findagrave.com,

trying to cause you any trouble," said Luce, looking the man in the eyes.

The stranger shook his hand but didn't say much. Then Andrews started hustling the three carousers out of the door. Noting that she wasn't making the stranger leave, Luce asked if he was her boyfriend. She indicated that he was, but he wasn't sure if that was true or just a way of getting them to move along.

It could have been just the end of another night at Fagiani's, but it wasn't. For one thing, the usual police drive-by didn't happen; otherwise, the officer would have noticed that a little later in the evening the Cadillac was gone but the doors weren't padlocked.

However, it wasn't until the next morning when Muriel Fagiani received a call from her mother that the horrible truth about how the rest of the night had gone began to make itself known. Her mother said she'd just received a call from the Napa State Hospital; her sister hadn't reported to work or phoned in sick. "Go check on her."

Muriel was puzzled; that wasn't like Anita who was always punctual and never missed work without letting somebody know why. She drove over to his sister's apartment but the Cadillac was missing and no one was home. She then decided to check the bar.

When she arrived, Muriel saw that the front door was missing its padlock, which was odd. She walked in and noted that the counter was wiped down and spotless and that all of the bar stools were neatly lined up—except for an ashtray on the far end and one stool that was out of line.

Then she noticed that two swinging doors leading to the storeroom, normally always open, were closed. She pushed through them and discovered why. The half-naked body of her sister lay on the floor in a pool of blood.

II

July-August 1974

When Napa police officer Joe Moore responded to the call for help at 9:04 a.m. he arrived to find Muriel Fagiani in a state of shock. "I think my sister's been raped," she said and pointed to the storeroom.

Moore walked into the room and immediately saw that Andrews was dead, but she had put up a hell of a fight. There was broken glass and blood everywhere—splattered on the walls, dripping down the cases of beer and mixers, and pooling on the floor beneath the victim's upper body. He secured the area and waited for assistance; meanwhile a BOLO, or "be on the lookout," was issued for the missing Cadillac.

Criminalist Peter Barnett arrived at 10:45 a.m. to collect evidence and record what he saw that would be relevant to putting a homicide case together. The DA's office didn't have the money for a full-time crime scene investigator so they hired Barnett, who lived in the Bay Area, to process major crimes scenes.

He noted that the bar counter was wiped spic and span except for an ashtray containing a single cigarette butt, a shot glass, and a spoon, all of which he bagged as potential evidence. Unlike the other stools, which were all neatly lined up beneath the counter, the stool in front of the ashtray had been moved out, as if someone had been sitting at it.

The bloody floor where Anita's body was found and outlined in white. Photo courtesy of the Napa County District Attorney's Office.

The sink behind the bar counter was also clean and empty except for a screwdriver sitting on the drain. It had been placed there wet and left a rust mark. Each of the three basins contained a small amount of water; the water in the middle one tested positive for blood.

A crumpled towel lay on the floor beneath the sink. There didn't appear to be any blood stains on it, but Barnett collected it too, as well as the screwdriver, and beer and alcohol bottles from the trash.

There were blood stains on the bar floor about two feet from the doors leading into the storeroom. Inside the room, Andrews lay on her back. Her clothes were torn, punctured by a sharp object, and partly removed. Her pants and underwear had been yanked off her right leg but remained on her left leg; her blouse had been opened and the bra pulled down. She still had one of her high heels on, though the other was found behind the counter, but was not wearing her watch, ring or any other jewelry. Nor could investigators locate her purse, credit cards or car keys.

Bloody footprints made by a man's shoe led from the storeroom to an upstairs office which contained a now-empty cash box and safe. He'd apparently dropped some of the coins on his way back down the stairs. Another bloody shoeprint was located just inside the front door of the bar.

While investigators were still going over the crime scene, David Luce arrived at the bar. He'd heard what happened and wanted to tell them about the previous night. He described the stranger as looking to be in his mid-30s, with a "flattened" hairstyle and thin lips.

After leaving the bar about 9:30, he said he and his friends had gone to dinner. When he walked past the bar an hour or so later, he noticed that the lights were off, the door closed and the Cadillac was gone.

The autopsy performed the next day revealed that Anita Andrews had been subjected to an attack of intense savagery and rage. Due to glass in her hair and cut on her scalp, as well as blood on the floor leading into the storeroom, the investigators surmised that she had been struck on the back of the head with a bottle while she was behind the counter, then dragged into the room.

However, while she might have been stunned at first, she fought valiantly for her life. Her nose was broken and other bruises attested to the closed-fist punches she took. But eventually she'd been overpowered. Her attacker stabbed her thirteen times, mostly in her chest, with the screwdriver found in the storeroom sink. He then tore her clothes off and attempted to rape her though the autopsy couldn't determine if he'd accomplished the act.

Word of Andrews' murder spread like wildfire through Napa. But who would have done such a thing to the popular bartender? And what happened to her Cadillac, which had disappeared along with her purse?

Blood splatter evidence from the Andrews murder scene. Photo courtesy of the Napa County District Attorney's Office.

Answering those questions was tasked to Napa police detectives John Bailey and Robert Jarecki. Thanks to Luce, suspicion immediately centered on the flirtatious man at the end of the bar. But who was he?

Luce and his two friends told police he was a stranger and they'd never seen him before. Just a drifter. But others thought the description of the suspect sounded like a welder Anita knew. And still others thought it described the boyfriend who worked for the carnival.

As the detectives chased each lead, they were unaware that the drifter-welder-carnival worker might all be one and the same man. This was in part because Andrews' daughter, Donna Hawkins, didn't tell them about the last time she'd talked to her mother on the telephone.

Hawkins, 23 years old and living in Walnut Creek about twenty-five miles away, had spoken to Andrews a week earlier when Hawkins called to a cancel a dinner date. During the conversation, her mom said she was fed up with her sometimes boyfriend, a mechanic who worked for a traveling carnival. Anita said he'd run up a $400 telephone bill at her apartment. He'd left his tools in the back of her Cadillac, but she wasn't giving them back until he paid her.

In addition to the telephone call between Andrews and Hawkins, the aftermath surrounding the murder of Anita Andrews was filled with other what-ifs. What if the night patrolman hadn't missed his pass by the bar and noticed that the padlock was missing on the door but the Cadillac was gone? He might have discovered Andrews' body many hours earlier and, perhaps, the killer wouldn't have had such a head start.

And Andrews' former neighbor, Joseph Silva, who was supposed to go out to dinner with her the night before, wondered what if he'd stopped by for a drink. He may have stayed and escorted Anita to her car, or discouraged the killer just with his presence. But he hadn't and it haunted him. As the investigation wore on without any apparent progress, he and a friend even checked out the parking lots at the Oakland and San Francisco airports looking for her Cadillac.

Bailey and Jarecki canvassed the neighborhood, asking if anybody had noticed anything, or anyone unusual. They scoured records of other rapes, robberies and murders to see if they could find anything that look similar to what happened at Fagiani's.

They came up with one name, Liston Beal. He'd checked into the Connor Hotel on July 10 and then checked out the next morning and left town. The hotel manager thought Beal had been acting weird when he checked out.

Even Luce and his friends were potential suspects. They'd been at the bar. Maybe they'd made up the stranger to cover themselves. But their stories checked out.

There was so little to go on. Those were the days before computers would make it easier for law enforcement agencies to share or receive information, so it was a month before the Napa detectives learned there was a hit on Andrews' credit card. Sometime before midnight on the night of the murder, a tan Cadillac pulled into a Sacramento truck stop off Highway 99, sixty miles northwest of Napa.

Paul Griener was the attendant on duty when the driver asked politely for ten dollars worth of gas. As he filled the tank, the 36-year-old Griener noticed a purse on the back seat and that the driver had covered his lap with a blue towel that appeared to be stained with blood. *Why the towel*, he thought and considered asking. But the driver didn't seem nervous; in fact, he would describe the driver to police as "calm, cool and collected."

So Griener let it go. Nor did he balk when the driver gave him a credit card with a woman's name on it. The man said it was his wife's card and signed it "A.E. Andrews" before pulling out and heading south.[2]

---

2   Sam Whiting, "Napa Bar Is a Reminder of Old Murder," *San Francisco Chronicle*, Nov. 17, 1989

However, where the driver went was anybody's guess. The Cadillac disappeared and never would be located.

After nearly two months of intense investigation, the Napa detectives had to admit that the case had gone stone cold dead. The evidence—a few bottles with fingerprints they couldn't match to anyone, a cigarette butt from the ashtray, broken glass from the bottle she'd been struck with, a towel the killer left on the floor of the storeroom, the murder weapon, a copy of the gas station receipt from Sacramento, and some photographs—was stored to await a break in the case.

III

August 30, 1974

Six weeks later after the murder of Anita Andrews and 1100 miles to the east, Michele Wallace was trudging down a gravel road beneath a backpack containing her sleeping bag, camping equipment, and her most prized possession, a 35 mm camera. Okie, her black, German shepherd dog, paced alongside laden with his own saddle pack. The 25-year-old woman was returning from a Labor Day weekend of hiking in a mountainous area of south-central Colorado known as Schofield Park.

As she walked, she must have had mixed feelings: a little melancholy, perhaps, about her plans to soon leave the mountains she loved, but also excited about the future. Earlier that summer, she had driven from South Carolina, where she had been photographing a rare bird species on the remote barrier islands, to her hometown of Chicago for her brother George Jr.'s wedding. There she regaled her family and friends, such as her best friend Donna Campeglia, with tales of her latest adventure—camping in the marshlands for a week waiting for a nest of eggs to hatch, covering the lower portions of her legs with tin cans as an improvised defense against rattlesnakes.

"She's got more balls than I ever had," her father, George Sr., remarked to his wife, Maggie, as they shook their heads and laughed over Michele's escapades.

At 5-feet-6 and 120 pounds, and much stronger than she appeared though a recent broken collarbone still bothered her. She seemed fearless to her friends and family. She'd once taken a job exercising polo ponies for a Chicago club, dashing full tilt across the fields. Later, she worked on a ranch, helping castrate young bulls at roundup time. She took up rock climbing and tried skydiving. She enrolled in martial arts classes. There was nothing a boy could do, her father boasted to friends, that she couldn't.

In her mid-20s, Michele was also a beautiful young woman, with rich chocolate eyes and delicate features. She often wore her long, dark hair in two thick braids.

Michele Wallace was 25 years old when she disappeared.
Photo courtesy of Donna Campeglia.

At her brother's wedding, Michele told her parents that she would be moving on to Colorado to spend the rest of the summer taking photographs of the Rocky Mountains. Then in the fall, she would return to North Carolina for her first professional photography assignment, chronicling the lives of the people who lived deep in the mountains there.

It was an isolated, backward world where moonshiners still plied their trade and the locals mistrusted strangers, she said, but she wasn't worried about her own safety. Highways and housing developments were pushing ever closer to their homes, and soon the hill people would be carried away by the tide of civilization. She wanted to make a record *"before they're gone."* Her idea was good enough to win her a government grant, but first she wanted to spend the summer in the mountains of Colorado.

So Michele moved to Gunnison, a small town with about 3,500 residents, in Gunnison County. It wasn't hard to see why: The town was surrounded by some of the most beautiful and rugged country in all of Colorado. It was set in a wide valley through which the Gunnison River flowed. The valley floor was covered with miles of scrubby, knee-high brush and stunted juniper trees interspersed with the cultivated fields of working ranches. Enormous cottonwood trees lined the banks of the river.

In the mountains, however, the landscape changed dramatically. Rangeland and cottonwoods gave way to steep, rocky slopes blanketed by forests thick with pine, fir, and groves of quaking aspen. The area was a Mecca for fishermen and hunters, who every fall more than doubled Gunnison County's population as they traipsed about the hills dressed in fluorescent orange. It was also a magnet for young people drawn to the area's outdoor recreational activities, including nearby Crested Butte ski area, 28 miles north of Gunnison.

Michele fit right in with the outdoor enthusiasts. She was well liked if somewhat quiet. A few of her acquaintances later said they thought of her as lonely, or lost, as if constantly searching for something. But their perceptions may have been clouded by hindsight because in 1974, Michele Wallace had her whole life to look forward to. Her parents had bought her the red 1973 Mazda station wagon with the South Carolina license plates, and her father paid for the insurance. Otherwise she supported herself that summer by working as a flagger for a highway construction crew.

It was how she met her roommate, Theresa Erikson, another flagger. The two young women and Okie moved into a house that had been converted into apartments across the street from the Gunnison County courthouse.

Michele had acquired the dog, named for the Okefenokee Swamp in southern Georgia, fully grown a year earlier. He was something of an enigma; he could be fiercely protective of his mistress or docile as a lamb. If young men came to visit, Okie usually went berserk. The girls had to chain him in the backyard or lock him in the kitchen, where he would continue to snarl and try to get back to Michele for as long as the visitor remained. When Michele visited her family in Chicago for her brother's wedding, he bristled if her father gave her a hug. However, when Michele and Okie visited the home of Theresa's parents in Montrose, some forty miles west of Gunnison, the dog took to Theresa's father like an old friend.

Near the end of August, Michele called her mother. Theresa was going out of town to a wedding, and Michele had decided to take a backpacking trip. It would be her last chance before she left for North Carolina. Michele informed her mother that she was leaving on the twenty-seventh. She said she might not return until September 2, but not to worry;

she was taking Okie with her and would be careful. "I'll call you as soon as I get back," she promised.

Some parents might have worried, but the Wallaces believed that their daughter knew how to take care of herself. Michele was well aware that the mountains could be dangerous, especially for someone alone and beyond help in case of an accident. She minimized the risks by letting people know where she was going, as well as when she expected to get back. She also had top-flight camping equipment and a large dog for protection.

Michele had a number of nearby areas to choose from for her trip. Fate, however, took her to Schofield Park, another ten miles beyond Crested Butte. Arriving in the area, she parked her car near the town of Gothic, a biological research station inhabited by only a few people, and walked a mile or so up the road to where a hiking trail began. She spent the next three days hiking and taking photographs: photographs of the mountains; photographs of Okie with his red dog pack; photographs of wildflowers and mountain wildlife.

On the fourth day, August 30, a Friday, Michele decided she was ready to return to Gunnison and, in a few short weeks, get on with the rest of her life. She packed her gear, settled Okie's pack on him, and strapped into her own for the march back to her car.

Michele's dog, Okie, was shot by a rancher after her disappearance. Photo taken by Michele Wallace

It was late afternoon when she reached the trailhead and the road to Gothic. As she left the trail, a beat-up car came wheezing up to her and stopped. Two men were inside. The driver offered her a beer.

Hot and grubby from her days in the mountains, Michele smiled and reached for the offered bottle. Not much of a drinker, she took only a sip before handing it back.

"We're only going up the road a bit and will be back in a few minutes if you want a ride," the driver told her.

"That'd be great," she said and waved as they chugged off.

A few minutes later, the men were back. A tire was going flat, they said, but they would probably make it to Gothic if she still wanted a ride. Michelle and Okie jumped in the back.

They had hardly gone a hundred yards when there was a loud clang. The driver got out and looked under the car. He got back in proclaiming it just wasn't his day; a rock had punched a hole in his oil pan. They all laughed. "How about I give you a ride when we get to Gothic?" Michele offered.

When they reached her car, the driver of the other vehicle got in the backseat with Okie. He looked like a ranch hand, tanned and weathered beyond his years. "I'm Chuck," he said.

"And I'm Roy," the other man added as he climbed in. He was the taller of the two and not bad-looking, even if his dishwater blond hair was thinning as he approached middle age. He smiled and shut the door, and said, "Thanks for the lift."

On the way back to Gunnison, Chuck made friends with the dog, who licked his face and then drooled on his lap for most of the trip. Roy and the girl were talking up front, but he couldn't hear much of what was said.

It was early evening when they arrived back in Gunnison outside the Columbine Bar. Chuck was surprised to hear Roy ask the girl if she would mind driving him a few blocks to his truck.

That's strange, Chuck thought; *I didn't know he had a truck.*" They'd been driving around, goofing off and boozing it up mostly, in his old rattletrap for two days since meeting in the Columbine. He thought about not letting the girl go off alone with Roy, but whiskey called so he decided he needed a drink more than he needed to be chivalrous.

Roy stepped out of the car to let Chuck exit. "I'll be back in a bit," he said to his confused drinking buddy; then he got back in the girl's car. It would several weeks before the two men would see each other again and under much different circumstances.

Michele Wallace, on the other hand, was never seen alive again.[3]

---

3   Steve Jackson, *No Stone Unturned* (WildBluePress, May 2015), Kindle Edition

IV

September 2, 1974

The fear in Margaret Wallace's voice was palpable. "Have you heard from Michele," she asked. "She always calls on Sunday, but she didn't call. And now it's Monday."

Donna Campeglia didn't know quite how to respond. Her best friend, her spiritual twin, Michele Wallace was living in Gunnison, Colorado, a long ways from Riverside, Illinois and they hadn't talked in a month. They mostly wrote letters and the last she'd heard Michele was excited to be living in the mountains and happy to have a job working for a highway crew.

It was unusual for Michele to miss her weekly check in with her mother. Still, Donna wasn't terribly alarmed; her friend tended to march to her own drummer and there were all sorts of plausible reasons she'd missed her call. For instance, Michele was always trekking around in the mountains with her dog, she could have met up with some other campers and decided to spend an extra couple of days exploring. Or maybe she was dating a new guy and was head-over-heels and not thinking about needing to call her mom. Or, well to be honest, Michele could be something of a "space cadet" and just forgot.

Other than her mom, nobody knew Michele better than Donna. They met when they were 13 years old in the girls' bathroom at Riverside Middle School as they were applying fresh mascara side-by-side at the mirror. It was ironic that Michele who would come to epitomize the Earth Mother-type, applied makeup when she was a teenager as though her life depended on it. "I have to go apply the plastic surgery," she'd say and away they'd head for the mirrors.

From the day they met, they were rarely apart. The two girls looked alike with soulful brown eyes and dark hair. Their birthdays were six days apart—Michele's was April 13 and Donna's the 19th—and kindred spirits. Donna was more gregarious, while Michele was content with Donna's friendship and that of their other best friend, Kathy Pransky. But with Donna driving, Michele was always up for an adventure or a party as long as they were together. She was what Donna's thought of as "a real Good-Time Charlie," always smiling, always joking, rarely serious.

They lived in a community where nothing bad ever happened; at least not of the criminal sort. Donna and her parents were in Riverside, a designed community known for its many parks and winding tree-lined streets. Michele, her parents, and brother George Jr. lived in North Riverside which wasn't quite as fairytale-like but she was right across the street from a forest preserve where she'd walk her dog— she always had a dog—without fear any time of the day or night.

After high school, Michele had been off to see the world while Donna got a job. Over the next few years, they'd see each other when Michele came home from wherever she had been living—Spain, Utah, or beloved mountains in Colorado. Or Donna would go see her. When Donna began vagabonding herself and went to live in Florida for a little while, "Mush" as she was known to family and friends, visited her. And in between they wrote dozens of letters.

There was something unsettled about Michele, as though she was always searching for something. Once when Donna was visiting her friend in Aspen, Colorado, Michele's boyfriend, a Frenchman named Gerard summed it up. *"Michele you are never present,"* he said. *"When you're eating you're thinking of going for a walk; when you're walking you're thinking of being somewhere else. You're always dreaming of something."*

Such comments didn't bother Michele. She'd just smile and go on dreaming.

The hardest part about visiting her for Donna was when they had to part. It was always a scene with both of them in tears. When it was time for Donna to leave Aspen after that trip, she got up early to take the bus to the airport. Michele was sleeping in another room so Donna packed as quietly as she could and left. She didn't want to say goodbye.

Sitting in the bus station, waiting to board, Donna thought she'd made a clean getaway. But as she was looking out the window at the snow-covered mountains, there came Michele, trudging through the drifts in her cowboy boots and eating a yogurt out of the plastic container without a spoon. She looked like Annie Oakley with her braids and outfit and lack of makeup, no longer the teen who couldn't live without her mascara.

Michele explained that she wasn't about to let her go without saying goodbye. So they stood there, arms wrapped around each other, crying until Donna finally had to get on the bus and leave her friend standing in the snow waving as tears streaked both of their faces.

That was Michele. Warm. Loving. Life-affirming. About the only thing that had ever really knocked her down was when their friend, Kathy Pransky, died in a car accident a few years earlier. Kathy, married and the mother of a young daughter, was killed in a traffic accident.

Kathy's death had devastated Michel and seemed to weigh her down like nothing else ever had. The Good-Time Charlie disappeared. And though she remained a loving, carefree spirit, a sadness seemed to linger over her.

Tall, blonde and outgoing, Margaret had married and had children young. Now she lived vicariously through her daughter. She encouraged Mush to travel and live the life of adventure she'd wanted, listening raptly to the stories her daughter brought home or divulged in their weekly telephone conversations.

Her father, George Sr., while he'd brag about Michele's exploits to friends, wasn't as big a fan of his daughter's sometimes harrowing accounts of her life. But "Mush" had always been independent and inclined to go against the grain, so with her mother's blessing, there was nothing much he could do about it.

As the summer of 1974 came to a close, the Wallaces thought they had it made. They had been married thirty-four years and were still in love. George's Italian restaurant was a success; the money was rolling in. Best of all, the kids were doing okay. Their son was married to a nice girl and, finally, out of the house. And Michele, a happy, confident girl, was embarked on what promised to be a wonderful journey through life.

The Wallaces were ecstatic that their daughter, an unfocused student for most of her young adulthood, seemed to have finally found something in photography that she would stay with. She had a real talent for it, both nature and "art" pieces, like the self-portrait she had taken while still a student at a photography school.

The black-and-white photograph was grainy and highly contrasted. It appeared to have been taken in winter when the leaves had fallen from the thin, dark trees of a city park. In the photograph, the slender silhouette of a young woman, Michele, stood in a clearing turned toward a bright light coming up over a hill in the background.

George Wallace thought it was a powerful photograph, almost disturbingly so, though he couldn't say why it made him feel that way. Then Michele didn't call on September 1 as she had promised.

"I'm sure she's fine," Donna Campeglia told Michele's mom. "She'll call soon."

V

September 3, 1974

The woman on the phone with the Gunnison County Sheriff's Office was absolutely certain something had happened to her daughter who she said had been backpacking in the area. "She didn't call Sunday when she was supposed to," the woman, who'd identified herself as Margaret Wallace, said.

"Maybe she just forgot to call or decided to camp an extra day," the Sheriff's Office dispatcher suggested.

"Not my daughter," Margaret replied. "She always calls when she says she will." She insisted that a search begin immediately. "She was going to be in the Schofield Park area."

Although there was nothing unusual about one of the area's young outdoor enthusiasts losing track of time in the mountains, or not checking in with their parents, the next morning, Gunnison County Undersheriff Steve Fry stopped by Michele's apartment just to see if she'd returned. But she wasn't there nor was her roommate, Theresa Erikson.

Fry frowned. Schofield Park was rugged country. The girl could have been injured and was waiting for help. He decided to call the Mt. Crested Butte Police Department and ask if someone could drive up to Gothic and look around for her car.

They checked the next day. But there was no sign of Michele or her car near Gothic.

When Michele still hadn't returned home by the following morning, and with Maggie Wallace calling for frequent reports, Fry and his boss, Gunnison County Sheriff Claude Porterfield, decided it was time to get serious about the missing girl. A massive search mission was launched by the Gunnison County SO with the assistance of the Civil Air Patrol, Monarch Search and Rescue Team, Mt. Crested Butte Police Department, Crested Butte Marshal's Office, deputies from neighboring Pitkin County, and numerous civilian volunteers.

Officially, Michele was listed as a missing person, but after several days of air and ground searches, Porterfield and Fry worried that she was more than missing. There was still no trace of her—not even her car, which should have stuck out like a bright, red sore thumb.

Fry returned to Michele's apartment and met with Theresa Erikson, who had returned. He asked her to identify Michele's possessions. "Only the things that she alone used," he said. Erikson handed over a brush and eyeglasses.

Just 24 years old and working on what would become his first major case, Fry did everything by the book. He carefully packaged, sealed, and identified each piece of evidence and placed them in the basement evidence room of the sheriff's office, not knowing if his diligence would someday pay off.

On September 6, Chuck Matthews was listening to the radio as he sat with the other ranch hands at the kitchen table of his boss, waiting for breakfast. The morning news was led by a story about a missing girl. Matthews nearly choked on his coffee when he heard the description of the girl, her dog, her car, and her last known whereabouts: Schofield Park.

Matthews realized that they were describing the young woman who had given him and *"Roy"* a ride to Gunnison on August 30.

Why, he thought, *I rode in the backseat of the red Mazda station wagon with that same dog.* He called the sheriff's office and gave the deputy who answered a brief description of meeting a girl who sounded like their missing person. The last time he had seen her was outside the Columbine Bar as she drove off with a guy he had met the day before. "Said his name was Roy … and that he worked for a sheep rancher in the Schofield Park area."

Matthews told the deputy that after his drinking buddy said he'd be right back and then left with the girl. He'd waited until 9 p.m. for Roy to return in his truck and give him a lift back to the ranch where he worked. But when Roy didn't come back, Matthews called another friend to come get him. He went home and thought no more about Roy, the girl, or her dog.

The next morning, he said, his friend took him to his car near Gothic so he could pick up his rifle and saddle. He noticed that Roy's toolbox was still in the car, so he left it there in case he came back for it.

Matthews's story wasn't what the sheriff's investigators wanted to hear. If he was to be believed, Michele had made it back to Gunnison but disappeared in the company of a man she did not know. In fact, nobody seemed to know who this Roy might be. Or where.

The news got worse the next day when Bob Niccoli, a rancher who lived ten miles south of Crested Butte, called the sheriff's office to report having killed a dog matching the description of the missing girl's German shepherd. The dog was chasing his cattle on September 4, when he shot and then buried the animal.

A deputy and Michele's cousin, Debbie Fountain, who lived in Denver and had come to Gunnison to help with the search, were dispatched to Niccoli's ranch. He took them to the field where he had buried the dog. But they didn't have to dig the animal up; he had kept the dog's collar, on which hung a tag with both the dog's and Michele's names on it.

It was further evidence that something had happened to Michele, that she hadn't simply picked up and moved on. Other people called to say they had seen the dog wandering in the area since August 31. Still more reported seeing girl backpackers, some of whom had dogs with them, in the Schofield Park area. They were all checked but none panned out; there were a lot of female hikers in the mountains.

Among the people they talked to was a young couple who remembered a middle-aged man they met on a trail who had a teen-aged girl with him. "He was kind of a slick-talking guy," the male in the couple recalled for the police. But the girl, who didn't speak and seemed subdued, was obviously too young to have been Michele.

On September 11, based on Chuck Matthews' recollection that Roy said he'd worked for a sheep rancher who grazed his stock in Schofield Park, the sheriff's investigators located Frank Spadafora. Yeah, the rancher acknowledged, he'd hired a Roy, a Roy Melanson, to be exact. He noted that his former employee didn't own a vehicle or much else for that matter. "I had to give him an old coat," he added, "and bought him a sleepin' bag to use." He'd had to fire him, but heard he had been living since in a Schofield Park cabin "with a bunch of hippies."

Up to now, the searchers and police had hoped that Michele was all right. Injured, maybe, waiting for rescue, but alive somewhere in the mountains around Schofield Park. Now they feared something worse had happened to her. Something to do with this Roy Melanson.[4]

---

4   Steve Jackson, *No Stone Unturned* (WildBluePress, May 2015), Kindle Edition

VI

Thirty-seven-years-old, Roy Melanson was a six-foot-one, 190-pound drifter with thinning hair and remarkably large hands. He was also a nightmare for unsuspecting women.

Born on February 13, 1937 in Breauxbridge, Louisiana, he was already well-known to law enforcement in southern Texas and Louisiana before his twentieth birthday. In August 1956, he was given a two-year suspended sentence "with supervision" for forgery and impersonating a federal officer in Corpus Christi, Texas. Apparently the supervision wasn't enough to stop him from committing a burglary in Louisiana for which he was sentenced to four years in the Louisiana State Penitentiary in December of that year. He was paroled after serving one year then proceeded to rack up more burglary charges in the towns of Orange and Port Arthur, Texas until they finally put him back in the Huntsville penitentiary for two years.

While it's doubtful he kept his nose clean in the interim, Melanson was accused of another crime within six months of getting out of prison. This time it wasn't just burglary.

In June 1961, he violently attempted to rape his first cousin in Pinehurst, Texas. He wasn't caught and arrested until November and then it took another year to convict him. He was then sentenced to twelve years in Huntsville but served only a little more than five years before he was released in July 1970.

Again it's anybody's guess what crimes he committed over the next two years—the police would have their suspicions later—but in August 1972 he was arrested for raping a woman in Orange, Texas. At his preliminary hearing, a proceeding to determine if there was enough evidence to go to trial, the woman testified that on the evening of August 8, 1972, she'd been on her way to a club when her car got a flat tire. Two men in a pickup truck stopped to offer assistance.

The driver, who said his name was Roy, was stocky with a beer belly. The passenger was younger, around 22, slender, and had short hair. The two men checked her spare tire, found that it was also flat and offered to drive her to get it fixed.

On the way, Roy said he needed to change trucks and then drove to a house where they left the young male passenger off. Roy put the tire in a different truck and the woman got in with him to get the tire fixed.

Instead, she testified, Roy drove to a secluded area where he "lunged" at her. He acted like she expected his advance and told her he was "going to fuck" her. She resisted but the more she fought, the more violent he became as he described what he was going to do to her.

Roy Melanson in a photograph from the 1970s. Photo courtesy of Gunnison County District Attorney's Office.

Roy punched her in the face with a closed fist, she said, which stunned her. However, she continued to resist until he twisted her arm back and pinned her down. He then pulled her pants off one leg and down to the knee of the other before raping and sodomizing her. Forcing her to perform other sexual acts, he talked to her throughout, telling her to "respect" his wishes as he sexually assaulted her for more than an hour.

After Roy finished, she testified, "he just sat there," at which point she decided to try to humor him, hoping she might outwit him. She made him laugh and offered him some tissue to clean himself, which she threw the tissue out the window along with her torn underwear so that it could be found later.

Allowing her to put her pants back on, Roy started apologizing, she said. Eventually, he drove to a gas station and arranged for someone to fix the tire. He then took her back to her car and changed the tire while she memorized his license plate number. When he was done, he apologized again for attacking her.

Back in their own cars, an acquaintance of the woman saw her and stopped to see if she was okay. Roy took off and was later arrested after she gave his license plate number to the police and described how to find the tissue and torn underwear.

During the preliminary hearing, a problem for the prosecution arose when the woman was asked to point out the person who had been driving the truck that stopped to assist her. Melanson was sitting in the courtroom, as was the young male passenger. The woman identified the young male, however it wasn't clear if she'd heard the question correctly and thought she'd been asked to identify the passenger.

In any event, the judge decided that the prosecution has presented enough evidence to bind the case over to trial. However, Melanson made bail and skipped town.

Two more years passed with Melanson managing to stay under the radar as far as coming to the attention of law enforcement while living in various towns in Texas and Louisiana with a woman he impregnated.

Then in February 1974, he was accused of brutally raping another woman. The 17-year-old victim told police that her attacker had first played the part of a Good Samaritan when he pulled into a gas station where she'd stopped to look for gas. There was a gas shortage at the time and the station was out. However, Melanson told her he knew where to find some, but once he had her alone, he abducted her. He then raped her before tying up and taking her to Louisiana where he continued raping her over a period of several days while threatening to kill her. She eventually talked him into letting her go.

The teenager was able to identify Melanson who had showed her his driver's license. However, she had a nervous breakdown and was sent to a psychiatric hospital. In the meantime, Melanson fled the area with his pregnant girlfriend.

In March 1974, Melanson was living with his girlfriend in a motel in Tucson, Arizona when they got in an argument and he left her. Where he went next wouldn't come to light for many years. However, on July 16 he was in Denver, Colorado where he visited a pawn shop and then caught a Trailways bus to Grand Junction, a small city on the western side of the state off Interstate 70 and almost to the Utah border.

Two weeks later, he was sitting in a Grand Junction bar when he got to talking to 40-year-old Frank Spadafora who said he had a sheep ranch in Somerset, near the town of Crested Butte. Spadafora complained that while he had a couple of Basque herders to watch the sheep, he needed someone to shoot coyotes that were preying on his flocks in their summer range in Schofield Park, a beautiful but rugged area high in the mountains.

A world-class bullshitter, Melanson convinced the sheep rancher that he was just the man for the killing. It was a perfect setup for him. He had nothing more than the clothes on his back, but now not only did he get free use of a rustic but serviceable cabin in a remote and beautiful part of the country, Spadafora loaned him a rifle and sleeping bag.

Melanson, however, didn't spend a lot of time working, especially after he discovered the Burton family. Lucille Burton and her five daughters were spending a few weeks of their summer in a cabin in Schofield Park while Lucille's husband remained in Pueblo. The log cabin had been in the family for several generations and wasn't much more than four walls, a roof, and a floor. But it was soon home, sweet home to Melanson.

Melanson was glib and worldly. He claimed to speak fluent French and soon had the girls and their mother enthralled with his stories. It was obvious he enjoyed the company of any young woman, even gallantly offering to take a friend of one of the girls, who had come for a visit, for a horseback ride. Nobody remarked on the fact that after they returned, the girl was quiet and subdued.

Of all the women, Melanson took a particular interest in 14-year-old Sally Burton. He began to spend so much time with her and not doing his job that on August 17, Spadafora fired him and took back the gun and sleeping bag he had loaned.

Melanson shrugged and moved in with his new friends. Such were his charms that a week later, when it was time for the Burton family to return to Pueblo, Melanson talked Sally's mom into leaving the teenager, 23 years his junior, with him.

It wasn't long before Sally saw at least part of what lurked beneath Melanson's charm. He kept her a virtual prisoner in the cabin. If she questioned his authority, he'd lunge as though to strike her, and then laugh as she cringed away. When he wanted sex, he demanded sex. If she protested that she wasn't in the mood, he got angry and insisted. She soon learned that if she didn't go along, he would force her anyway, and so, afraid of his temper, she acquiesced. Adding insult to injury, he gave her a case of body lice.

Sally, however, was lucky. She got to leave. On August 28, Melanson let her catch a bus home to Pueblo; however, he said, he'd be joining her soon. The next day, Melanson decided to head for Pueblo, 160 miles to the east. He didn't own a car, so after hitchhiking the 28-miles to Gunnison he purchased a bus ticket.

With time to kill before the bus departed, he decided to throw back a few drinks at the Columbine Bar. Maybe find a new sucker for his lies ... or something even better. He accomplished the first when Chuck Matthews, a Vietnam combat veteran and ranchhand, sat down next to him and they struck up a conversation.

Over a half-dozen beers, Melanson told the older man that he owned a cabin, horses, and land in Schofield Park. He was having trouble of late with a bear that was harassing his animals, he said. He didn't suppose Matthews knew of anybody who could help him out with the bear.

Well, sure, Matthews said. He had a rifle back at his place. He'd fetch it and a saddle; then they could go get a couple of

Melanson's horses and together they'd get rid of that danged old bear. The two men staggered off to Matthews's beat-up car, took off for the ranch where Matthews worked, and picked up the rifle and saddle. They left for the Burton cabin, but by the time they arrived it was too dark to look around for the "bear."

The next morning, Melanson had another story. He'd rented his horses to a guy who obviously hadn't returned them. The other man owed him money, too. The guy lived in a cabin on Kebler Pass. Would Matthews mind driving him there? They might just spot that pesky bear along the way.

As the crow flies, Schofield Pass is only about ten miles north of Kebler Pass. But 12,809-foot Mount Baldy stands between them, and the only way to get from one to the other was to go back to Crested Butte and then head west up the other fork in the road to Kebler. Melanson knew the drive. To get from the Schofield summer range to Spadafora's place in Somerset, he'd been over Kebler Pass several times.

Matthews agreed to the new plan. So after tossing Melanson's toolbox in the car (in case of engine trouble) and stopping to buy more beer, they were rattling down the road again.

On Kebler Pass, however, Melanson couldn't seem to locate the cabin, his horses, or the guy who owed him money. To make matters worse, Matthews's car kept breaking down. If it wasn't something with the engine, then it was a tire gone flat, and even the spare had a slow leak. Still, Melanson wanted to explore several dirt logging roads that ran south from the main road. He said that if he couldn't find the man who owed him money, he at least wanted to find that bear.

It was worrisome, considering they didn't see a soul on the logging roads, and couldn't expect much help if the car broke down permanently. But Matthews, fortified with beer, gamely tried to help his new friend.

Driving along one such road, about ten miles up the pass from Crested Butte, Melanson suddenly asked him to pull over; he thought he'd seen something. Maybe the bear.

Matthews did as asked, then got out of the car. "Hand me the rifle," Melanson said. Again Matthews complied and even turned his back on his pal and walked over to the edge of the road where Melanson had pointed. It was pretty country with steep north-facing slopes covered by coniferous trees and aspen tumbling down to a flatter area through which a creek ran along the edge of a meadow.

When Matthews turned back around, Melanson had a strange look on his face, as if he had just thought better of something. "Let's go," Melanson said and tossed the rifle back into the car.

The pair made it back to Crested Butte, where they stopped at a gas station to see if they could fix the leak in the tire. It couldn't be fixed, so they pumped it up, bought another six-pack of beer, and headed up the road to the Burton cabin. That's when he and Matthews met the girl and her dog.

The next morning, August 31, Melanson walked into the J. C. Penny's department store in downtown Gunnison. He bought a cotton dress shirt and polyester slacks, paying with a check on which he wrote "For new clothes."

He then left the store and got into the red Mazda station wagon belonging to Michele Wallace. Even though the store was only a block in one direction from the Gunnison Police Department and a block in another from the Gunnison County Sheriff's Office, he was unconcerned about being stopped in the car. He knew there was no one to report it stolen.

Melanson drove to Pueblo and went to a bar where he called the Burton house. He learned that Lucille and her husband were out of town. One of Sally's older sisters,

Becky, was left in charge and said she didn't want Melanson to come over. He stashed the Mazda and went to the Burton's home anyway.

After spending the night with Sally, he got another sister to drive them to where he had parked the Mazda. He explained that a friend from Boulder had left it for him to use.

Melanson seemed to be doing much better than when Sally had last seen him a couple of days earlier. He was wearing new clothes and had acquired all sorts of new possessions. He had new camping equipment, including a backpack, sleeping bag, and stove. And he had a nice camera, even allowing Sally to take his photograph as he lay smiling on a couch behind one of her friends.

On September 3, the day Michele's mother reported her missing, Melanson drove the "borrowed" Mazda to a pawnshop, where he pawned the camera and a lens. He signed the pawn ticket using his real name. However, when he checked into a motel with Sally later that afternoon, he signed in under the name Allan King, giving an address of General Delivery, Nile, South Carolina. He didn't provide a license plate number when registering, but the owner of the motel took it down later that evening anyway.

Soon Melanson was on the road again. Leaving Sally behind, he went first to Kansas. Then he was off to Cedar Falls, Iowa, where on September 8, he pawned a sleeping bag and Kelty backpack at Ken's Pawn Shop. From Iowa, he headed south to Elk City, Oklahoma, where he met 34-year-old Thurman Gene Wilder.

Melanson was again drinking in a bar when Wilder came in and the two men started talking. Wilder said he was looking for work as a heavy-equipment operator. He had transportation—a white Cadillac he was mighty proud of—but no job opportunities.

"It's your lucky day," Melanson said. It just so happened that he had a friend who owned a big construction firm in Pueblo, Colorado. He was sure he could get Wilder a job driving a bulldozer.

The next day, they headed west, Melanson in the Mazda with South Carolina plates; Wilder in his 1963 Cadillac. They got as far as Amarillo, Texas, where they stopped for a cold beer at The Hard Hat Lounge. Melanson announced that he needed to take the Mazda to a garage for repairs. First, though, he had Wilder assist him with transferring his stuff from the Mazda to the trunk of Wilder's Cadillac. Then, telling his new friend to wait for him in the bar, Melanson left.

A half hour later, Melanson returned, saying he had had to leave the car at the garage. It was going to take a few days for repairs. "We'll have to go to Colorado in your car," he said, "and pick mine up when we come back this way."

On September 12, the day after the Gunnison Sheriff's Department investigator talked to Frank Spadafora, an anonymous caller reported a suspicious white Cadillac with two men in it prowling around a Pueblo high school. "It keeps coming and going," the caller said. "I think they may be selling drugs."

Officer Russ Laino responded and pulled over the Cadillac. Melanson was driving and said he and his friend, Thurman, were just waiting to give one of the students, Sally Burton, a ride home from school. He handed over a Texas driver's license; Wilder handed over his as well.

Laino went back to his car to run the licenses through the police computer to check for any outstanding warrants. "The computer's down," he was told. He read off the license numbers to be checked later and went back to where the two men sat in the Cadillac and handed back their licenses.

It was a half hour later when Laino got a sudden message from dispatch. The computer was back up: The guy from Texas was wanted for aggravated rape. Alarmed about having left the suspect, Roy Melanson, at a high school filled with young women, the officer stepped on it. But the white Cadillac was nowhere to be seen.

A BOLO was issued, and a couple of hours later, Laino spotted the white Cadillac in front of a motel. He checked with the motel manager, who said one of the men had checked in under the last name of Allen. Laino called for backup and Melanson and Wilder were arrested at gunpoint.

Wilder gave the police permission to search his car. There they found a number of things that belonged to Michele Wallace. That included a vehicle registration for a 1973 Mazda, her driver's license, her Amoco Motor Club membership card, and an insurance card in the name of George Wallace. In the car, the police also recovered camping equipment and a dog pack, as well as a Mazda tool kit.

At the jail, Melanson was stripped. In his pants were two pawn tickets: one for a sleeping bag and backpack; the second for a camera. They also recovered an unused bus ticket from Gunnison to Pueblo—and a set of Mazda car keys.

The Pueblo detectives were sharp. One of them recalled that a BOLO had been issued by the Gunnison Sheriff's Department for a red Mazda station wagon owned by a Michele Wallace. They didn't know what they had yet, but they knew that there was no good reason Melanson would have the young woman's personal effects.

They called Gunnison and learned about the search. Undersheriff Fry said they had a warrant out for Melanson's arrest on check fraud charges from another case. "Hold him until I can get down there," he said.

The evidence from Wilder's car and Melanson's pockets was handed over to Officer J. E. Trujillo. Meanwhile, Wilder told detectives Jimmy Smalley and Bob Silva about meeting Melanson and how they had left a red Mazda station wagon in Amarillo.

Unaware of what Wilder was saying, Melanson told Smalley that he'd never been in Michele Wallace's car. He said he didn't even know what a Mazda looked like.

However, the Amarillo police soon turned up the car. It had been abandoned one block from The Hard Hat Lounge. Amarillo PD crime lab technician G. W. Dickerson checked out the car for evidence of foul play but found none.

In separate interviews, Melanson and Wilder both mentioned that the former had spent time with the Burton family in Pueblo. Melanson even admitted to having a relationship with Sally, although he denied it was sexual, since that would have landed him in more hot water for having sex with a minor.

Other detectives interviewed Sally Burton, who admitted knowing Melanson, saying she had met him near her family's cabin. She told them about Melanson's arrival in Pueblo and the little red car she and her sisters had traveled in. She even pointed out the room at the Bell Motel where she spent the night of September 3 with Melanson. And yes, she said, they did have sex.

More detectives talked to the motel owner, who remembered Melanson, though under the name Allan King. He still had the license plate number he took off the Mazda. It belonged to the car owned by Michele Wallace.

In the meantime, Melanson was being raked over the coals regarding Michele by Smalley and Silva. At first he said he didn't know her. Then he seemed to remember that she may have been one of a group of "hippies" who had shown up at his cabin in Schofield Park before moving on.

On September 13, Undersheriff Fry drove to Pueblo, where he met with the Pueblo detectives, who brought him up to date on everything they had learned. Fry asked to speak to Wilder and Melanson. He began with Wilder, who told him about meeting Melanson. "What kind of car was Roy Melanson driving?" Fry asked.

"A red Mazda station wagon," Wilder said.

"Did you ever hear Roy say anything about a girl by the name of Michele Wallace?"

"No," Wilder replied, shaking his head. "Never."

Fry finished with Wilder and asked that Melanson be brought in. A few minutes later, he was told that Melanson didn't want to talk to him but did want to talk to the FBI.

FBI Special Agent Lad Scroggins arrived and talked to Melanson for several hours. At first, the ex-con stuck to his story. But with the agent pressing, he suddenly "remembered." Yes, he had met Michele Wallace. He had gone into a bar with her to have a drink. "We left the dog tied outside," he said. Melanson said he made an excuse to borrow her car. Then he left. "And that was the last I seen of her," he said.

Neither Scroggins nor the other detectives were fooled by Melanson's confession. As an ex-con, he knew that taking a stolen car across state lines was a federal offense—the only crime in this case the FBI would have jurisdiction over. They figured he was hoping that the FBI would charge him for the car theft, with a maximum penalty of five years in prison, and in the intervening time period, the Michele Wallace case would be forgotten.

The next day, Fry arrested Melanson for fraud. He was suspected of having broken into a car in the Schofield Park area and then forging his name and cashing checks that belonged to the car's owner. Fry took possession of the evidence related to the Wallace case, including her camera from the Pueblo pawn shop, and put his prisoner in the back of his county car.

The drive back to Gunnison was uneventful. Melanson was sticking to his story: The last time he saw Michele Wallace, she was alive and drinking in a bar.

Melanson was booked into the Gunnison County Jail that night. The next afternoon, Sheriff Porterfield and Fry questioned him about Michele Wallace. Again, he denied having anything to do with her disappearance.

"What are you going to do when she shows up back in Chicago?" he retorted in response to their questions. "I'll be in the clear then."

Melanson asked what was going to happen with the fraud charge. When they replied that it would be up to the courts, he indicated that he was through with the interview but that he would think about it and "decide if I want to say anymore."

He decided against. But the investigators were hearing a lot more about Melanson from other law enforcement agencies. He was a suspect in three rapes in Texas, and was under indictment for one in February of that year when he fled the state.

Texas authorities also wanted to talk to him about a murdered woman whose body had been found in a field; they knew he had been in the area at the time, but they had little else to go on. And Louisiana police wanted to question him about a series of strangulation murders in that state.

Fry made arrangements to retrieve Michele's sleeping bag and backpack from Cedar Falls. On September 20, Chuck Matthews was asked to report to the Gunnison jail. They wanted to ask him more questions and see if he could identify Roy Melanson as the "Roy" he had met the day before Michele Wallace disappeared.

There was soon no question about that. Melanson was being led from his cell when Matthews came in. "That's him," Matthews yelled and with his fists clenched, advanced at the other man. He might be a drunk, but he had served his country honorably and wouldn't abide a man who attacked women. "You son of a bitch," he shouted "You did somethin' to that poor girl!"

"I didn't do nothin'," Melanson snarled back.

The two men moved toward each other. Matthews was smaller, but he was more than willing to mix it up with Melanson. Deputies quickly stepped between them.

Matthews settled down quickly in an interview room and gave a more detailed account of his time with Melanson and Michele Wallace. Undersheriff Fry took particular note when Matthews said they had been in the Kebler Pass area, about eight miles up and had taken several side excursions on tracks south of the main road. He recalled one in particular because they drove through two streams to get to the place where Melanson had him stop and hand him the rifle.

There was something curious, Matthews added as the interview drew to a close. The morning after Melanson left him at the bar and drove off with the girl, a friend gave him a lift back to his car to retrieve his rifle and saddle. Melanson's toolbox was still in the car, he said, and that's where he left it. But when he returned to the car the following day, the toolbox was gone. "That means he stuck around long enough that morning to come back for his tools."

With Matthews's positive identification, the Gunnison County Sheriff investigators were certain they had the right man and that Michele Wallace had been murdered. It was unlikely he had taken her very far, which meant her body was somewhere in the mountains. But they couldn't find her, and without a body the District Attorney was reluctant to attempt a murder trial.

After killing Michele Wallace, Roy Melanson stole her camera. This photograph of him lying on a couch two days after the murder was the last image on the film. Photo courtesy of Gunnison County District Attorney's Office.

The circumstance became even more aggravating when, a week after picking up Melanson in Pueblo, Fry had the film in Michele's camera developed. Most of the photographs were from her camping trip. But the last frame on the roll was a photograph of the suspect lying on the couch at the Burton home, a young girl sitting in front of him reading a newspaper; Melanson had a smirk on his face as though daring the investigators to catch him.[5]

---

5   Steve Jackson, *No Stone Unturned* (WildBluePress, May 2015), Kindle Edition

VII

October 1974

Donna Campeglia's heart didn't give up on Michele being alive until she heard about her dog from Maggie Wallace. Her brain had warned her that it was over when her friend didn't call during that first week and the searchers couldn't find her. But if the dog had been wandering free before it was shot, she knew that something terrible had happened to Michele.

A few day later, that was confirmed when George Sr. called. Michele had last been seen in the company of a known rapist, and that he'd shown up later with her car and pawned her camera.

He must have threatened the dog, Donna thought. *She would have never just let Okie go; she would have done anything to protect him.*

Devastated, Donna thought about the last time she'd seen Michele who'd come to visit her. Donna was living in Tucson with a mutual friend, Gary, who Michele had once dated.

Michele was still recovering from a broken collarbone and unable to lift her arm when she got in the shower one day. *"Hey kid,"* she'd called out for Donna. Referring to each other as 'Hey kid,' was one of their jokes since junior high, and they'd continued to use it, including in their frequent letters.

When Donna walked into the bathroom, Michele pulled aside the shower curtain. She had a typical crazy grin on her face and a razor in one hand. She wanted help shaving her armpits. *"You're the only person I could ask to do this,"* she'd pleaded with a laugh.

"Oh for God's sake," Donna had laughed back, but she'd done as asked.

As usual, they'd hugged and cried when it was time for Michele to leave Tucson, though neither knew it would be the last time. It was after that trip that Michele had moved to Gunnison, Colorado and out of her life forever. Thinking about Michele being attacked, Donna knew her friend would have had a difficult time defending herself because of her collarbone.

Calling with the news about Okie was the last time Donna heard from Maggie Wallace. As hundreds of searchers combed thousands of square miles in Colorado from the ground and the air, the Wallaces told each other to keep their hopes up. She might have been injured on the trail or slid off a treacherous mountain road in her car. But day followed day with no word, no trace of their daughter.

They struggled to avoid accepting the unacceptable. Not death. Not Michele. She was too tough, too smart, too able to die. But with each day that passed, hope began to slip beneath the surface of their bravado like a drowning man.

The waiting was hard on all of them, but particularly Maggie. She was always on the telephone: calling the sheriff; calling the FBI; calling the governor of Colorado. A brother who was a colonel in the Air Force had jets fly over the area. She called anyone she thought might help, but no one could.

What news they got was always bad and nothing came along to make it better. A convicted rapist claimed to have left Michele and her dog alive and well in Gunnison when he took off with her car. The Wallaces knew the story was a lie; Michele rarely drank, and she certainly wouldn't have loaned her car, with her camera in it, to a stranger. But there was no evidence he had killed her—no evidence that she was even dead.

Still, Maggie knew, and she deteriorated day by day. Hollow-eyed and dazed, she cried and wandered around the house like a lost child. She pored over photographs of Michele, caressing the likeness of a face she would never again touch in the flesh. Six weeks after Michele disappeared, the Colorado authorities called and asked for Michele's dental records. It meant they had given up hope of finding her alive. They also said that there was an early snowstorm moving in and they were going to have to call off the search.

Maggie reached the end of the rope she was grasping. One night soon after, the Wallaces were in bed. Maggie was reading and George was going over the books from his restaurant. "Would you like some tea?" Maggie asked, getting up.

It was a strange question for the time of night, but George, aware of his wife's fragile state, humored her. "What the hell," he smiled, "if you're up and around, sure."

When she returned with the tea, he took a sip and wrinkled his nose. It tasted terrible. "Where in the hell did you get this tea?" he teased. "Have you been keeping it in a pot for a week or something?"

Maggie didn't say anything but took the cup from him and left the room. He shrugged and turned out the lights. He was almost asleep when she returned a few minutes later and lay down beside him.

George woke the next morning knowing that something was wrong. You don't sleep next to a person for thirty-four years without becoming attuned to their breathing and heartbeat, the warmth of their body beneath the sheets. But on this morning, though he could feel the weight of Maggie beside him, there was no hint of her gentle breathing or the quiet thumping of her heart through the mattress.

With tears already welling in his eyes, he sat up and looked at his wife. She appeared peaceful, more at rest than any time since Michele had disappeared—still beautiful. But she was cold when he reached over to touch her, and he knew that she had gone on to join Michele.

Maggie Wallace had taken an overdose of barbiturates with her tea. Waiting had been too great a burden for her to bear, but in dying she placed a heavier burden still on the husband she loved. *"If you ever find our daughter, please bury her next to me,"* she wrote in the note she left for him to find.

George promised he would try. As he stood next to Maggie's grave a few days later, he swore that someday he would face the man he now believed had killed his daughter and his wife. He would look him in the eye and send him back to hell.

But not all of his anger was directed at Melanson. He was disappointed with the Gunnison County Sheriff's Office as well. If they had found Michele's body, he believed his wife would have still been alive. She would have been grief-stricken, yes, but he was convinced that it was the terrible not-knowing that had pushed her into taking her own life. He called the sheriff and said as much.

That bastard, Roy Melanson, was telling the cops to go screw themselves and to get out of his face. George volunteered to fly to Gunnison and shoot "the mad dog" in his cell.

Back in Colorado, there was nothing much anyone could say to placate George Wallace. But he was from Chicago and had no concept of the sheer immensity of the land into which

Michele had disappeared. Thousands of man-hours had been spent in the search.

They had a suspect, but he wasn't talking. They had a lot of circumstantial evidence, but the district attorney wasn't willing to prosecute.

"There's no way we can file charges without finding her body, or evidence that she met with foul play," said Lynn French, the deputy district attorney prosecuting the fraud charges.

Maybe that fall, during hunting season, someone would stumble across her body, the district attorney suggested. But when winter came to the high country, dumping hundreds of inches of snow, the search for Michele Wallace froze as well.[6]

After Maggie killed herself, George Sr. called Donna. Almost out of his mind trying to deal with how quickly his life had disintegrated, he was angry at his wife. It was bad enough that Michele was gone, but she didn't care enough about him or their son and took her own life? It was more than he could take.

Donna tried to console him. She told him that he needed to go on for his son's sake. That someday Michele would be found and he'd get to keep his promise to bury her next to her mother.

But it was like the blind leading the blind. As Donna tried to help her friend's father, she kept thinking in her grief *nobody is helping me.*

---

6   Steve Jackson, *No Stone Unturned* (WildBluePress, May 2015), Kindle Edition

VIII

November 1975

The young woman on the witness stand in the Texas courtroom looked over at the defense table as she described the man who'd raped her almost two years earlier as "looking like an old cowboy ... his hair was greasy and slicked back." She pointed at Roy Melanson "that's him."

It was Melanson's second trial of 1975. In March, he'd been tried for fraud in Gunnison, Colorado, accused of having broken into the car of Alice Moss in Schofield Park in August 1974 and then cashed checks he found inside. But everyone knew that fraud charges weren't what were keeping Melanson in the Gunnison County Jail while Texas authorities were waiting to prosecute him for rape. It was the hope that searchers could find the body of Michele Wallace and then he'd be charged with murder.

The day of Melanson's trial in Gunnison arrived, but the prosecution's main witness, the victim, didn't show up. Although Moss was prepared to testify, the day before she was scheduled to appear at the trial, she received a telephone call at her home in Boulder, a six-hour drive from Gunnison. The woman on the other end of the line said she was the Gunnison County court clerk and that Moss didn't need to show up. She said a deal had been worked out.

Without the victim, Melanson's female public defender was able to convince the jury to acquit him. No one was able to determine who called the witness and told her not to come. But now there was no legal reason for Gunnison authorities to keep him in jail. So they'd shipped Melanson off to Texas.

Texas Ranger Haskel Taylor was there waiting for him. Taylor had been after Melanson since February 1974 for the rape of the 17-year-old woman he'd sexually assaulted in Texas and then transported to Louisiana where he'd continued terrorizing and raping her.

Taylor thought Melanson was guilty of a lot more than raping that woman, or the other rapes that were on his record. The Texas Ranger believed he was also responsible for the beating death of a woman whose body had been found in a field. Melanson was the last person seen with that victim, too, but Taylor didn't have enough evidence to bring a case against him.

However, there was plenty of evidence now, the most damning of which was the testimony of his victim, who'd recovered enough from the horror of her ordeal to take the stand. She recalled for the jury how she'd pulled into a gas station that night in February 1974 only to find the station out of gas and closed. However, just as she was about to drive away, a man drove up in a truck and told her that he knew where to find gas.

As she was following the "old cowboy," she said, he'd suddenly pulled over and gestured that he needed help. He asked her to try to start his truck while he looked under the hood. But when she got in his truck, he shoved her down onto the floorboard and threatened to kill her if she tried to get up.

Melanson then drove to an empty field where he raped her several times. At some point another car drove past the field and she lunged for the horn and hit it, trying to get attract attention. But her assailant struck her, and then tied her up with her pantyhose and a rope before gagging her and blindfolding her.

After that Melanson seemed unsure of what he was going to do with her next. He drove her to a garbage dump where he raped her again and repeatedly threatened to kill her. He then took her to another location, forced her into another car, and then transported her across the border into Louisiana, stopping in a remote swamp. There he raped her repeatedly.

"He said if I didn't enjoy it, he would kill me," she testified. Unable to ejaculate, he seemed "frustrated and mad and forceful."

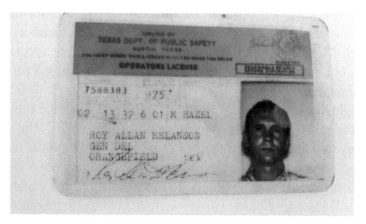

*Roy Melanson's driver's license. Photo courtesy of
Gunnison County District Attorney's Office.*

Melanson's assault on the girl lasted for a couple of days. He kept the pantyhose around her throat and if she cried or resisted him, he'd tighten the garrote. After the last time he raped her, she decided that if she wanted to survive she needed to talk him down. The young woman testified that she told him she'd tell her mother that she'd run away, and that she'd be believed because there were problems at home.

Melanson reacted as though he thought they might now become a couple. He said he'd take her to a pay phone where she could call her father. As they drove back to Texas, he even showed her his driver's license. He then confessed that he was the uncle of a girl she went to school with and that he'd been stalking her.

Still, before letting her go, Melanson threatened her again. "He said he would kill me if I reported him."

It didn't take long for the jury in Texas to find Melanson guilty of rape. Then under a "three strikes" habitual offender provision in the Texas legal system, he was automatically sentenced to life in prison.

Back in Colorado, those who believed that Melanson had killed Michele, a murder that had led to the suicide of her mother, were relieved to hear about the life sentence. At least they'd be able to find him in a Texas prison when they found her body and could prosecute him for murder.

Unfortunately that wasn't true. And the consequence was horrific.

IX

July 1979

The search for Michele Wallace was the largest ever conducted in Colorado in terms of personnel and resources. More than 400 volunteers and law enforcement personnel participated in the months after she first disappeared. In all, 164 hours were flown by air searchers. Another 5,000 man-hours were spent walking a 150- to 200-square-mile area on foot; and an additional 300 square miles were covered by vehicles.

However, it was also a lot of ground to cover. Gunnison County, in south-central Colorado, is 3,266 square miles of mostly uninhabited wilderness. And it was as if the earth had opened up and swallowed the mortal remains of Michele Wallace.

Then on July 26, 1979, a hiker named Thomas Kolz was walking along a logging track off the main road over Kebler Pass. It was a little-used path, just wide enough for one-way traffic and intersected twice by a shallow stream. The day was hot, and Kolz had stopped to rest when he spotted something dark lying in the middle of where the road forked. It was a mass of hair, parted down the middle into two long, dark braids.

Kolz returned to Gunnison and gave the hair to the sheriff's office. Suddenly, Michele Wallace was back in the news. The hair was sent to the Colorado Bureau of Investigation. There criminalist Nelson Jennett confirmed that the hair was definitely human. But without a specimen known to have come from Michele, he couldn't positively identify it as hers.

Another search was launched, this time concentrated near where Kolz had found the hair. It narrowed the search area considerably, but that hardly made it easy. The tree-covered hillsides were so steep that searchers mostly had to walk along the roads and peer over the edge.

In the end, the searchers again went home empty-handed. No one could say how the hair got to the middle of the logging road. It could have been thrown from a car window, or a scavenger might have carried it there from miles away. The searchers wondered how long the hair had been on the road, and why no one had seen it before.

The hair remained hidden away in an evidence box for six long years until the day Deputy Scott Jackson opened the box and showed the braids to a 33-year-old rookie detective named Kathy Young. No one knew it yet, but it was the day Melanson's evil ways began to catch up to him.

Young had moved to Gunnison a year after Michele Wallace disappeared. She was 19 years old then and wanted to spend a summer camping and hiking before returning to California to attend college. The name Michele Wallace had come up wherever people gathered—at softball games and picnics, in bars, and around campfires. Adventurous young women like Kathy were warned about going into the wilderness alone. It didn't necessarily stop them, but it sure was on their minds when they met strangers on the trail.

Prior to coming to Gunnison, Young never imagined working in law enforcement. Her first experience was as the city's animal control officer in 1977. She soon learned that the term meant more than dogcatcher in a rural setting, such as when some pranksters at Western State College left a bawling calf on the third floor of one of the dormitories. She and an officer had to carry the hefty creature down three flights of stairs and then spent several hours trying to locate the unbranded calf's owner.

Another aspect of the job wasn't quite so appealing. Dogs allowed to run loose by their owners sometimes chased cattle. In this part of the country, ranchers were legally within their rights to shoot dogs that endangered their livelihood. Young was taken aback. As a California girl, she wasn't familiar with laws meant to protect livestock in ranch country.

The more Young was around police officers, the more interested she became in becoming one. In 1978, she was accepted as the first female officer on the Gunnison Police Department. It wasn't easy. A typical response from a drunk on the street was, "Screw you; you're not a real cop." She always felt as if she had to go the extra mile.

Young put her law enforcement career on hold after she married and had two sons. In 1985, she joined the sheriff's department, again as the first female deputy on the force. Three years later, she became the county's first female investigator.

A short time later, Detective Young got a call from Roland Turner, the chief of the Mt. Crested Butte Police Department. He had been digging through some old files and thought there was a case she might be interested in: "a girl that disappeared up here in nineteen seventy-four, named Michele Wallace."

*Investigator Kathy Young of the Gunnison County
Sheriff's Office. Photo courtesy of Kathy Young.*

Turner said he had been cleared to talk to her by her boss, Sheriff Ric Murdie. "This case has been bothering me for a long time," Turner said. "I'd appreciate it if you'd take a look."

Young asked Murdie for permission to work on the old case. He said to go ahead as long as it didn't interfere with her current workload. He knew that the disappearance of Michele Wallace had been hanging over his community for too long.

Murdie had been born in Gunnison, but his family had moved to Denver when he was a boy. He had joined the Marines out of high school and then returned to Denver and joined the police force. After thirteen years with the Denver Police Department, however, he tired of the big city violence and crime and returned to Gunnison. In 1986, he ran for sheriff and won.

One of the first things he had done was to create the position of investigator, the county version of a police detective, giving it to the man who was Young's predecessor. He had followed that by reviewing the department's unsolved cases. He had seen the Michele Wallace reports. No one in law enforcement liked knowing that a case of that sort was unresolved. A guy getting away with murder was something he took personally.

Experience told him the case was solvable. The district attorney at the time had declined to prosecute without a body, but there was a new man in office, Mike Stern, and maybe he'd be willing to take a chance. Murdie had heard of body-less homicides being prosecuted successfully—not often, but it had been done. He harbored no illusions about the possibility of finding Michele Wallace's remains after more than fifteen years.

The problem was freeing the time to allow his only investigator to pursue such an old case. Gunnison had grown a lot in the intervening years, and there was plenty for his deputies and investigator to do. When Young requested permission to pursue the case, however, he felt he had to agree.

Young began talking to Deputy Jackson. He told her about the search after the hair was found on Kebler Pass. "It's still in the evidence room," he said. "You have to see it, Kathy."

When they pulled it out of the box, still sealed in a plastic bag, Young was startled. Jackson hadn't told her that the hair was still in braids. She had pinned a photograph of Michele up on her office wall; she was wearing braids. Now here was a tangible link between the girl in the photograph and the case that she was so completely immersing herself in.

Young, and Jackson, when he could spare time from his patrol duties, began to pore over the 15-year-old files. The more she saw, the less she understood why Roy Melanson had not been prosecuted.

There was the interview with Chuck Matthews. The description of the logging road he had taken with Melanson sounded as though it was near the same place where the hair was later found. She wondered if Melanson had planned to shoot Matthews when he got out of the car that day but had decided against it because of the condition of the car. It wouldn't do to break down in another man's car, near where the owner's body lay, she thought. Michele's car, on the other hand, was dependable. . . .

Young was curious about the dog, Okie. He had been shot and buried on the road north of Gunnison, nearly 20 miles from where the hair was discovered west of Crested Butte. Had Michele persuaded her killer to let the dog go? Or had the killer found a way to separate her from her protector and then taken her somewhere else to kill her? Maybe the dog wasn't as protective as he was made out to be. According to Matthews, Okie sat next to him all the way back to Gunnison with no problem, even licked the ranch hand's face.

Other old reports caught her eye. On April 30, 1975, just a few days after Melanson was shipped off to Texas, another Gunnison County inmate, John Paul Steele, told Undersheriff Fry that Melanson admitted killing Michele. *"He said he was glad that he wouldn't be around in the spring when y'all would start digging around for her,"* he said.

Steele had asked if they had found her dog.

"Yes," Fry said without volunteering any other information.

"Was it up north near Crested Butte?"

Fry said it was, but the dog was dead. Steele scowled and said, *"He said he didn't kill the dog."*

The undersheriff then told Steele that Melanson didn't kill the dog. The inmate's information was accurate and surprisingly detailed, such as when he noted that Melanson had told him that Michele had extensive dental work. *"He must have been real close to notice that,"* he added.

Melanson had told him that he dug a grave and poured lime over the body to speed decomposition before burying her. Even more gruesome, he claimed to have used an axe to knock out her teeth, to hinder identification if her body was discovered.

Young found a report that another inmate, Jack Hassig, had told Fry a similar story, including the part about Melanson talking about his alleged victim's dental work. She knew that Michele had indeed had extensive work done, including a gold molar.

Although others had described Melanson as a "slick talker" and "smooth," Melanson's mouth damned him too. Instead of just settling on the story he eventually concocted—that he'd left Michele alive and well at a bar and then took off in her car with her belongs—he lied about everything. He said he'd never met her. Or taken a ride in her car. And then he denied taking her belongings and her car; said he didn't even know what a Mazda looked like. All of which was demonstrably proved to be untrue and would come off to jurors as a man trying to cover his tracks.

"This is solvable," Young muttered.[7]

---

7   Steve Jackson, *No Stone Unturned* (WildBluePress, May 2015), Kindle Edition

XI

July 2, 1988

Even in a Texas prison, Melanson couldn't stay out of trouble. He was suspected of beating a young black man to death. But none of the other inmates wanted to be labeled a snitch, so he got away with it.

As it turned out "life in prison" didn't mean he was only going to leave the Huntsville penitentiary in a wooden box. A jailhouse lawyer, Melanson got his habitual offender statute over-turned. He was then resentenced to 33 years of which he served a little over twelve and was released without parole in March 1988.

After getting out, Melanson, now 51 years old, went to live in Port Arthur, staying with the mother of his son he'd once abandoned in Tucson and her current boyfriend. The couple was renting an apartment from Pauline Klumpp, a 51-year-old woman who owned the complex.

On July 2, Klumpp drove to the apartment to pick up a television that needed to be repaired. While there, she said she needed help with an air conditioner at her home. Melanson volunteered to assist and the two left in her car.

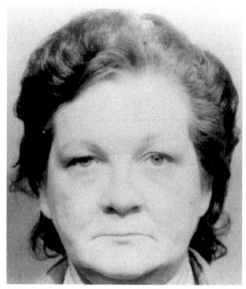

Pauline Klumpp disappeared in 1988. She was last seen in the company of Roy Melanson. Photo courtesy of Texas Rangers.

The next day Klumpp's car was found parked in front of a grocery store with the television still inside. However, she had disappeared.

And so did Roy Melanson.

XII

Walker, Louisiana
August 6, 1988

Four days after Pauline Klumpp disappeared, and 206 miles due east of Port Arthur, Vince LeJeune was starting to panic, as he turned his Ford F250 truck down the gravel road that led to the property where he and his fiancé, Charlotte Sauerwin, planned to build their dream home. There was nothing on it now but stumps, pulpwood pines and brush. It was getting dark, and he couldn't find her anywhere in town, so he'd decided to see if she'd driven out there to think about the house she wanted, as she sometimes did.

They'd argued the night before about the property, located a few miles out of the town of Walker where'd they'd both grown up. Charlotte was anxious to move from the little shack they lived in on her parents' place and into a trailer on the land until they could build a proper home. First, they needed to get the land cleared and leveled. That was going to take a minimum of $1,200, which he'd had a tough time getting together, especially as he kept spending his paychecks on other things, like a new motorcycle.

Getting the land ready to build on was becoming a real source of friction. Charlotte was getting frustrated, and he felt like she was nagging him. The previous night he'd been out in the garage working on the motorcycle when she began badgering him about it. *"Just let me handle it,"* he'd said, irritated.

However, she wouldn't let it drop. She said she'd met someone who claimed he could probably get it done a lot cheaper than what LeJeune had been told. She said she was going to meet the man the next day and take him to the property to show him around and get his estimate.

LeJeune decided he was tired of hearing about it. *"Do whatever you want,"* he grumbled.

Things were still tense when they went to bed. In the morning, she got up and made him lunch like she always did, then followed him to the door and locked it after he went out. He couldn't remember if they'd said *'I love you,'* or even *'goodbye,'* when he left for work.

They'd known each other since the 8th Grade when her best friend Sheila asked him to be Sheila's boyfriend. He'd actually dated both girls through junior and senior high school, and somehow they'd all stayed friends. There were only a few hundred kids in all of Walker High School and not much to do, except get together with classmates, talk someone old enough into buying them a few six-packs of beer, and then meet on the gravel road he was now driving down, build a bonfire and get drunk.

After high school, he and Charlotte had stayed in touch and even dated a little. He didn't graduate but had a good job repairing fuel storage tanks and traveled a lot throughout Louisiana, Texas, and Arkansas. They'd go out when he was in town, but there was no deep love or commitments. Not until he went to California to work for a few months in 1985 and found that he couldn't stop thinking about her, did he decide she was the girl for him. He came back to Louisiana and was happy to learn that she'd just broken up with her boyfriend. They were engaged a short time later.

The property wasn't the only source of contention for the young couple. They planned to get married in 1989, after he turned 25, but LeJeune sometimes worried if living in Walker and being married to him was going to be enough for Charlotte.

Charlotte Sauerwin and Vince LeJeune were engaged to be married when she was murdered in 1988. Photo courtesy of Vince LeJeune.

Located off Interstate 12 in Livingston Parish about 20 miles east of Baton Rouge, the town wasn't much more than a dot on a map. The one and only main drag boasted one traffic light, two convenience stores, and a fried chicken shack. With a population of less than 3,000, it was the sort of community where everybody knew everybody else, or knew somebody who knew everybody. There wasn't much that went on that the locals didn't hear about through the grapevine, though the facts might have changed, been ignored, or were absent by the time the gossips got through with them.

Charlotte said she wanted marriage, kids, and the all-American dream home with a nice front porch and the white picket fence. She also enjoyed traveling with him to his job sites and talked about seeing more of the world. Pretty and outgoing, she thought she might accomplish this through modeling. In fact, she'd recently accepted an invitation from a modeling agency in Baton Rogue for a photoshoot.

The modeling dream troubled LeJeune. He wanted her to be happy, but he also was scared that if she achieved her goal, it would be the end of them as a couple. He thought she'd be off to parts unknown and he'd be left in Livingston Parish. It was in his best interest to get the property cleared and the house built, but so far he'd only managed to save $900.

Still, by the time he got off work that day, he was over their fight. He didn't think it was any big deal, just the normal sort of spat between two 24-year-olds who didn't have a lot of money and or maturity. However, she wasn't home when he arrived home; so he grilled two steaks and waited.

Only when it started getting dark did he begin worrying. It wasn't like her to take off and not let him know where she was. She'd left her fiercely protective 65-pound pitbull dog at home, but he noticed she'd taken the little .380 Beretta semi-automatic handgun he'd given her. That in itself was unusual because she was afraid of the gun, having once accidentally discharged it and put a bullet into the floor. He wondered if it had to do with meeting the man she'd talked about. She was reserved around strangers and might have taken the gun as a precaution.

There wasn't a lot of crime of any sort in Walker. Sometimes a couple of good old boys would get drunk and there'd be a fistfight. That was about the extent of violent crimes—no shootings, no stabbings, no rapes. One of the few exceptions to that had devastated Charlotte's family many years before. LeJeune hadn't even met her yet when her brother was found sitting in a chair dead with a bullet wound to the back of his head. The police had ruled it suicide, but Charlotte's dad was convinced he'd been executed over a drug deal gone bad.

Still, that sort of thing was the exception, not the rule, so he wasn't thinking about Charlotte being the victim of foul play when he decided to go look for her. Maybe she'd had car trouble, or was still angry with him over the property. He walked over to her parent's house where her dad said he saw her leave about 2 p.m.

He then decided to drive over to Sheila's, who was still Charlotte's best friend. On the way, he called his friend Ricky, whose wife was also one of his fiancée's friends.

Ricky said he'd seen her that afternoon at the Laundromat talking to a stranger. "Something about getting your land cleared." He further reported that they'd gone outside to talk and he hadn't noticed if they left together.

Sheila also said that when she spoke to Charlotte earlier in the day, she was talking about meeting someone who was going to give her a good deal on clearing the property. "Have you looked for her out there?"

With everybody pointing that direction, LeJeune decided to drive out to the property. Charlotte sometimes liked to go out there to listen to her music and dream about her home. He didn't know why she'd still be out there after dark—maybe she'd had car trouble or got hurt and needed help—but it was all he had to go on. Turning onto the gravel road, he was disappointed not to see her car in his headlights. There was a little curve at the end of the road so he continued on, just in case.

Coming around the bend, he saw Charlotte's car was just off the road in the grass. He drove past and parked on the side of the road. Getting out of his truck, he grabbed a flashlight and walked over to her car to look in the windows. His heart skipped a beat when he saw the stereo and speakers had been removed. He understood that the car was now a crime scene and didn't open the door. However, he did put his extra key in the trunk lock and popped it open.

If somebody did something to her, he thought, *maybe they put her in the trunk.* She wasn't there.

Trying to calm himself, LeJeune lit a cigarette and began walking around calling her name. There was no answer.

Suddenly, a little ways down the road, he saw a car pull into a driveway and stop. He ran for his truck and threw it into reverse and began backing down the road. Panicking, he swerved and struck the side of Charlotte's car, but kept on going until he reached the other car whose driver he recognized as a local restaurant owner.

"I need help," he yelled as he exited his truck. "Call the police!"

The next few hours passed in a blur as deputies arrived from the Livingston Parish Sheriff's Office and a search began. Already he wouldn't remember, someone must have asked him if there was somebody they should call for him because his mother and father, as well as several friends arrived.

LeJeune wanted to help with the search but the deputies wouldn't let him so he was forced to wait. After a few hours, search dogs were brought to the scene. Then about 2 a.m., a deputy approached him. "We found her. She's deceased."

The deputy restrained LeJeune when he tried to push past him to go to where they'd found his fiancé. "I can't let you go," he said, "it's a crime scene now." He intimated that LeJeune wouldn't want to see what had happened to Charlotte.

However, LeJeune couldn't accept that. He and the deputy exchanged words, and it began to get heated. Finally, his dad took him aside in an effort to calm him down.

It was a nightmare. One that Vince LeJeune didn't realize was just beginning.

XIII

November 1989

Fifteen years after the event, the murder of Anita Andrews was again the subject of a newspaper article, when Sam Whiting, a reporter for the *San Francisco Chronicle,* wrote a piece under the headline "Napa Bar Is A Reminder of Old Murder."

However, as the article noted, it wasn't as though the residents of Napa needed a newspaper to remind them of what happened. Even if the mystery of who killed the popular bartender remained, there was no ignoring that a museum of sorts sat in the middle of downtown.

Over the years since the murder, Napa had evolved into a trendy wine-tourist destination; money and people with "progressive" ideas poured into the town changing everything. The fleabag hotel and several bars across the street were replaced with a scenic riverfront park and an upscale brew pub. A popular Mexican restaurant had sprung up on one side of the lounge and a nouveau frame shop occupied the building on the other side. Fagiani's remained unchanged.

When the police were finished combing the crime scene after her sister's murder, Muriel Fagiani padlocked the door, and closed the bar, leaving everything as it had been.

Bottles of booze still lined the wall behind the counter, beer waited in the fridge, more of both remained stacked in the storeroom, as well as nineteen bar stools, just one of them out of line. She also left the more sinister reminders of what happened on July 10, 1974—coins the killer had dropped on the staircase, and the shattered glass and blood on the walls and floor.

The interior of Fagiani's bar as it looked in July 1974. Photo courtesy of the Napa County District Attorney's Office.

In spite of the skyrocketing value of that piece of real estate, Muriel refused to sell the bar or allow it to be reopened. Fagiani's Cocktail Lounge, with its retro- red-and-white sign and funky tiled exterior stayed unchanged, closed for business, the windows boarded up, and the shadows inside left alone with their secrets. It even became a destination stop for tours of historical Napa where the horror of what took place was recounted in breathless detail.

Muriel shrugged when the *Chronicle* reporter asked what she was going to do with the building. *"I have no plans,"* she said.

However, she did have a purpose. She'd shut the place down to preserve the evidence in case there was something still in the bar that might someday help the police convict Anita's killer.

Blood splatter on the refrigerator in the Fagiani's storeroom. Photo courtesy of the Napa County District Attorney's Office.

Nor had Muriel been content to just leave the building as a reminder. Whenever there was a new police chief or mayor, or a detective she was meeting for the first time, she reminded them that her sister's murder was still unsolved.

"I have always been amazed," Fagiani told the reporter, *"that something like this could happen and no one could come up with anything."*

Fagiani wasn't the only one frustrated with the lack of progress. While working on his article, Whiting interviewed the two detectives who'd worked the case first, John Bailey and Robert Jarecki, as well as Jim Boitano, who was the District Attorney of Napa County at the time of the murder. They, too, had never forgotten the murder.

Boitano told the reporter that almost every day when he drove down mainstream he still asked himself, *"Why couldn't we solve that murder? ... It's tough to see somebody that I considered a friend brutally murdered, especially when it happened within feet of my office."*

Bailey, who had since retired from police work, told Whiting it was his most frustrating case in 25 years in law enforcement. *"Every time I go by the bar and see the lock on the door I think about it,"* he said.

Jarecki, a Captain with the police department, again raised a 'what-if' that had plagued the investigation from the beginning: the missed police drive-by. *"If the door without the lock had been seen, the body would have been found that night,"* he noted. *"Who knows what could have happened?"*

Boitano told Whiting that he had two different theories about the murderer and why he hadn't been caught. The first was that the killer himself had died shortly afterwards.

"But it couldn't have been an auto accident; we'd have the car," he said then surmised, *"The car might be in the bottom of the Sacramento River with the killer's body and the credit card."* The problem with that theory, he added however, was that after 1974 a series of droughts should have exposed the car, or brought up the body, if it was in the Sacramento River.

His second theory was that the killer had local ties but had driven to Sacramento and bought gas to throw investigators off his trail. *"Make it seem like an isolated drifter incident,"* he said. *"The killer is alive and out there, and there's got to be some tie to Napa through the State Hospital."*

Bailey shared Boitano's suspicions. *"It always kind of ate at me,"* said Bailey, who left the Napa force a year after the murder and later served 10 years as Tiburon Police Chief. *"The guy could have bought gas with cash. There was enough money in her purse."*

Bailey speculated that after leaving a paper trail at the gas station and heading south, as if to drive to Los Angeles, the murderer doubled back to the Napa area and was still living there. The car, he said, had probably been dismantled.

However, Jarecki stuck with the random crime scenario. *"Every indication is that it was a transient situation,"* he told Whiting. He admitted there were holes with his theory.

"How did the person who took the keys know which car was hers?" If the killer was a stranger, why did Anita allow him to stay when she ushered the other three men out of the bar?

The two detectives and prosecutor soon learned something new. While working on his story, Whiting talked to Anita's daughter, Debbie Hawkins, who'd been living in fear that her mother's killer was still in the Napa area. She told him that the sometimes boyfriend who worked for the carnival was also the welder/mechanic, which was news to the other men.

Apparently, up until that point, Bailey and Jarecki had believed that they were two different men.

"It was never relayed to us that the carnival worker was also a welder," Jarecki told Whiting, *"or that the carnival worker had his tools in the back of her car."* Nor was it known that Andrews had a current relationship with the man. *"If this had come out in the investigation, he would have been prime suspect No. 1. We've got to find out where this guy is now."*

Whiting noted that *"responding to fresh clues unearthed in the preparation of this article, Napa police have assigned the case high priority and put an investigator on it for the first time in 10 years."*

Eventually, the detectives learned the identity of the carnival mechanic. Unfortunately, like so many others, he turned out to be another dead-end. It looked like the case might never be solved.

XIV

Early 1990

Kathy Young was horrified. She'd just called the Texas Department of Corrections to inquire about Melanson and learned that he had been released in 1988. His "life" sentence had lasted 13 years.

Young could only wonder how many women had suffered as a result. It wasn't long before she found out. The Gunnison investigator contacted the legendary Texas Rangers in an attempt to locate Melanson's sexual assault victims. She wanted to know if there was anything about his attacks on them that might help link him to a murder case in Gunnison.

Young was put in contact with Ranger Haskel Taylor, who had spent a good number of years following the trail of Melanson. He was the one who had pursued him on the rape charges and extradited him from Colorado. However, there wasn't much he could tell her about Melanson's early years. The suspect had graduated from high school, where his grades were satisfactory if not spectacular. Apparently, his parents were dead.

Taylor provided her with Melanson's criminal record. He had never been able to find the earlier rape victims to interview them.

Melanson was a suspect in a number of killings, Taylor added. Besides the beating death of the young inmate in prison, there was a woman whose body had been found in a field after having been seen with Melanson. The police at the time hadn't had enough evidence for charges to be filed.

"More recently, he's the prime suspect in the disappearance of a Port Arthur woman," Taylor said and told her the story of Pauline Klumpp.

Taylor said he'd questioned Melanson about Klumpp. Just as he had in the Wallace case, he claimed to have left the woman safe and sound.

Young was somewhat relieved when Taylor told her that Melanson was back in prison. In 1989, he'd been arrested for burglary in Kentucky. He fled but authorities caught up to him, living on a ranch in Montana owned by a woman. He had convinced the woman that he was the wealthy owner of a ranch in Texas.

When he was arrested, Melanson was driving a small tan car with Texas plates and carrying a .380 Beretta with the serial numbers filed down. Taken back to Kentucky, Melanson, now 53 years old, was convicted of burglary and being a felon in possession of a gun. He was sentenced again as a habitual felony offender.

The habitual offender sentence was supposed to mean he would serve as much as twenty years in the Kentucky state penitentiary. However, Young was told by prison authorities there that Melanson would be up for parole in another five years or so with good behavior.

For the time being, Young knew where to find Melanson, but she didn't yet have enough for Murder to take to District Attorney Stern. She was going to have to locate as many of the former witnesses as she could and try to reconstruct the case.[8]

---

8   Steve Jackson, *No Stone Unturned* (WildBluePress, May 2015), Kindle Edition

XV

Late Spring 1991

It seemed like a recurring nightmare. Once again, Vince LeJeune found himself sitting in an interview room across from the dour faced Livingston Parish chief of detectives Kernie Foster. The big man had just told him that an anonymous caller claimed that LeJeune had confessed to the murder of his fiancée, Charlotte Sauerwin.

LeJeune sighed and shook his head. He was pretty sure he knew who the caller would have been. He'd just been through a bitter breakup with the mother of his infant daughter and she wasn't too happy with him. She was back using hard drugs. She wanted more child support, but wasn't willing to let him have visitation rights. This was just the sort of thing she'd do to get even.

However, it wasn't the first time he'd been accused of killing Charlotte. In fact, only a couple of days after her body was found, he'd realized with shock and horror that he was the prime suspect. Up until that point, he'd been in such a daze the first time that he didn't realize what the investigators were after when they, almost apologetically, said they needed to ask him a few questions. "You know, get as much information as we can," he was told.

However, they kept asking him to come back down to the sheriff's office and then kept asking the same questions, only using different words and phrases. Then if he got confused, or answered a little differently, they'd jump all over him. "That's not what you said before," they'd say as if he was changing his story. That's when he realized they thought he did it.

At first they tried to make a big deal about him sideswiping Charlotte's car, as if he'd run her off the road. They had to concede, however, that the damage showed he'd been driving in reverse.

Still, they continued to try to break him down, even showing him photographs of what happened to Charlotte. The killer had tied a rope around her neck and dragged her through the woods to a clear cut. There he'd raped and beat her so bad that he caved in the side of her face. He'd also strangled her and slit her throat.

When LeJeune saw the photographs his mind went red with thoughts of revenge. He couldn't believe that the police could suspect that he was even capable of such brutality. He understood wanting to catch the killer; he wanted revenge not just justice.

It was apparent that the investigators didn't have much else to go on. They'd had no luck tracking down the man from the Laundromat who his friend Ricky said he saw talking to Charlotte about clearing the property.

He'd been described by another witness, unknown to LeJeune, as in his 50s and claimed to be a Cajun from the Lafayette area, 75 miles to the east. However, the man and the small, tan- or light-colored car with out-of-state plates he was supposedly driving had disappeared.

The police even acted as if they thought the whole thing was made up by his friend Ricky to cover for him. Also, as though to say that the killer must have been local and knew the area was secluded, the police pointed out that after murdering Charlotte, the killer had taken the time to steal the stereo equipment out of the car. That, they said, meant he felt confident that he wasn't going to be discovered.

LeJeune tried to stay calm in the face of the thinly veiled accusations from the police interrogators. He knew they wanted him to slip up, say something they could twist, but he wasn't going to give it to them. Neither was he uncooperative. He never asked for a lawyer; never refused to come down to the station whenever they asked; never refused to answer their questions.

Still, no matter how many times he voluntarily answered their questions, they had not relented, especially Foster. There was no changing his mind. He was sure LeJeune was the killer and made it clear that he'd stay after him until he could prove it.

It was almost like a cruel game that nearly led to another homicide. This time, LeJeune would have been guilty.

At one point, the Livingston Parish SO investigators started playing LeJeune against his friends, especially Ricky. He and Ricky had grown up together hunting, fishing, and working on hot rod cars. Charlotte and Ricky's wife were good friends.

During one of his many interviews, LeJeune was asked if any of his friends dipped snuff.

"Well, yeah, all of them," he replied.

What about Ricky in particular? They asked the question as if it was significant, and proceeded to say that Ricky was being "evasive," not answering questions, and had refused to take a polygraph test. They also noted that he was one of the last people to see her according to his account of the Laundromat scene.

The seed of distrust was planted. It grew in LeJeune's mind until he believed his friend had murdered his fiancée. He put a handgun in his pants beneath his shirt and went to confront Ricky, pulling into his driveway hot and fast.

Ricky saw him coming and walked abruptly into the house. He came back out as his brother, Terry, roared up in his car and slid into the driveway. That struck LeJeune as suspicious. Foster had told him there could have been more than one killer, or that one guy did it and someone else was covering for him.

Everybody was tense, but nobody said anything. Then Ricky turned to go to his shack behind the house where he worked on car parts. LeJeune followed him.

Sure now that Ricky was the murderer, LeJeune intended to kill him. He slipped the gun out of his pants and aimed it at the back of his friend's head. He couldn't pull the trigger and put the gun away before Ricky turned back around.

Ricky said he and his brother wanted to go for a ride and check out where they were planning to hunt during deer season. LeJeune thought it was an excuse to take him into the woods to kill him.

So when they got into Ricky's four-wheel drive vehicle, LeJeune sat in the backseat. With his hand hovering near the gun, he thought about killing them both, but the trip ended without incident.

LeJeune realized later that he'd been acting on suspicions planted by the police and that Ricky and Terry had nothing to do with Charlotte's murder, but their friendship was never the same.

In fact, the "cruel game" ended other friendships as well, as he and his friends were all encouraged to look at each other as possible murderers. Some even told him later that they'd been asked to wear a "wire," to record conversations. They said they'd been told to get drunk with him and try to trick him into saying something incriminating.

As Foster continued to hound him, LeJeune told himself that the detective was just doing his job, and, of course, he was a suspect. Over time, he came to believe that the man had put on blinders, and he resented him for it.

The chief of detectives wasn't the only one who thought LeJeune killed Charlotte Sauerwin. Except for his family and a handful of his closest friends, the whole town seemed to believe it. Her family certainly did. They refused to talk to him and whenever he accidentally ran into her sister, Charlene, the woman would start trembling and act like she was going to die of fright.

The cloud hung over him everywhere he went in town, and there was nothing he could do to change it. He'd see someone he knew in a store and they'd simply stare at him or turn and hurry off the other way. He heard the whispered conversations, "That's the guy who killed his girlfriend."

Oh, he could have left and made a life for himself somewhere else. He still traveled a lot for work in Texas, Mississippi, and Arkansas. He always returned home. Walker was where his family lived, where he'd been born and raised … and fell in love. He wasn't the type to cut and run, especially when he wasn't guilty of anything.

Besides, running would just have confirmed what everybody thought. "This is my home," he told his friends and family. "I'm staying."

It wasn't always easy or pretty. There were dark times when his friends had to "talk him off the fence." He drank a lot and did a lot of drugs, especially with the girlfriend he'd just broken up with. They did them all—heroin, ecstasy, cocaine and pain pills—in a never-ending attempt to forget the past, the whispers, the accusations in people's eyes.

Their lifestyle changed when his girlfriend got pregnant. They both agreed that for the sake of the baby, they'd stop doing drugs. A healthy baby girl was born three days before his own birthday on December 20, 1990.

However, his girlfriend went right back to doing hardcore drugs. But LeJeune had found something better, his daughter. He wanted to be around for her and not as some drug-addled lowlife.

The child's mother wouldn't stop using drugs, so he left her, though it hurt because the court awarded her custody and wouldn't give him visitation rights. Bitter and vindictive, she wouldn't let him see the child. She wanted more child support, which he was willing to give her in exchange for visitation.

Instead, he was sure, she'd called the sheriff's office and said he confessed to killing Charlotte. Again he'd come down to the office, answered Foster's questions, and gone home. He determined that he wasn't going to let this thing beat him, not when he had a little girl to live for.

XVI

"You ever hear of the 'pig people'?"

Kathy Young frowned up at the tall man standing in the hallway of the Montrose County courthouse. She'd been working on the Wallace case whenever she could find time outside of her regular workload, and believed that she was getting close to making a case against Roy Melanson. The holdup was they still had not been able to locate Michele's remains despite the searches and the passage of time. Although the district attorney had finally said he might be willing to prosecute a body-less homicide case, it would make a difficult case that much tougher.

She'd just mentioned that obstacle to criminalist Nelson Jennett, who she'd serendipitously met in the hallway. In 1979, Jennett was the Colorado Bureau of Investigation agent who had confirmed that a "mass of hair in the form of two braids approximately twelve inches long" found on Kebler Pass was human. *Now he wants to know if I've heard about some pig people?*

She'd just spent the past two years or so running down every lead and witness she could find. On March 22, 1990, she found Jack Hassig, who was living in Montrose. He repeated the story Melanson had told him in jail about burying Michele near a stream and pouring a sack of lime into the grave. "He said he cut out her jaws, top and bottom, with an axe or a hatchet so she couldn't be identified."

Others weren't so easy to locate. Young spent months trying to find Chuck Matthews until someone recalled that he had a sister in the area. The sister told the detective that Chuck had moved to Truth or Consequences, New Mexico, so she drove there and interviewed the old ranch hand.

He was hazy about some of the chronology and names of places he had gone with Melanson, but he was clear about most things, including the part about his drinking partner driving off with the girl to "find his truck."

As a police officer, Young knew that she couldn't rule out Matthews as a suspect even if everything else pointed to Melanson. It didn't take long before she thought to herself, *He wasn't involved. ... He just isn't the kind of guy who attacks women.*

After all these years, Matthews was still angry at Melanson, recalling the confrontation at the sheriff's office —and maybe feeling a little ashamed that he had just stood there, anxious to get into the bar, when "that son of a bitch" drove off with the girl. He said he would be happy to return to Gunnison to testify. "Just tell me when."

Young also located Lucille Burton in Denver. She was in frail health but readily recalled the summer she and her daughters met Roy Melanson. There was one other thing she had never told anyone else. One of her daughters, the young girl who had accepted Melanson's offer to go horseback riding, later told her that he had raped her. The girl was afraid of him and had said nothing at the time.

Lucille Burton said her daughter, Sally, was living in California, so Young made arrangements to go and interview her. On the way, she stopped in Las Vegas to see Frank Spadafora, who had given up sheep ranching to run a small casino off the strip.

Spadafora didn't show at their prearranged meeting, so Young moved on to California to see Sally Burton. She encountered a mixed-up young woman who had been through a series of

disastrous relationships. She remembered Roy Melanson real well.

Yes, she said, her relationship with Melanson had been sexual— whether she wanted it that way or not. His moods could swing from one extreme to the next in an instant. He never hit her, but he always let her know who was in control and that she had better not cross him. "One time I wanted to leave the cabin, but he said I couldn't," Sally recalled. "He didn't say what he would do if I tried, but I saw his eyes and knew I wasn't goin' nowhere."

Burton recalled the red Mazda station wagon with all the camping equipment in the back, and said she would be willing to come back and testify if charges were ever filed.

On the way back to Colorado, Young called ahead to set up another appointment with Spadafora, who claimed to have mixed up the previous appointment time. She arrived in Las Vegas only to be stood up again.

When she returned to Gunnison, Young called the Las Vegas Police Department and reached a detective, Parker McManus. She started to explain what she was trying to do when he interrupted her.

"You know Punch McManus?" he asked.

Sure, Young said. Punch was a popular school teacher in Gunnison who had retired just a few years earlier.

"She's my mom," McManus said. "I grew up in Gunnison, and I remember when Michele Wallace disappeared." He said he would personally go "take care of the problem" with Frank Spadafora. The former sheepherder called the next day. He agreed to meet with Sheriff Murdie, who was going to Las Vegas on other business. This time he kept the appointment.

John Paul Steele, the former inmate who had told Fry a similar story to what Hassig had related, also took months to locate. Young finally found a parole officer in the state of Washington who gave her an old telephone number he had for Steele. The number was for a garage where Steele had worked as a mechanic. A woman answered and said Steele still worked there; in fact, she was his wife.

"He's not in any trouble," Young explained. "I just want to talk to him about an old case and a guy named Roy Melanson. Ask him to call collect."

Steele called back that evening. He remembered Melanson and related what he had told Fry many years before.

Young was impressed that the stories both Hassig and Steele told her remained consistent with their nearly 16-year-old statements. Their recollections of what Melanson had told them were almost exact.

As difficult as it was to locate some of the witnesses, there were two with whom she had no luck at all. They were dead. Kolz, the hiker who had found the hair, had died in a crash. Kolz's widow was still in the Montrose area, so Young talked to her about where they had been hiking that day.

Young heard that Thurman Gene Wilder also had died in a crash. The detective took no chances and persuaded a Louisiana State Trooper to go to the cemetery where Wilder was buried to check for his headstone. It was there, as was Wilder's body.

Young felt such efforts were important. Without a body, how were they supposed to prove that Michele Wallace was even dead, rather than living anonymously in some other part of the country? The prosecutors would be trying to prove a negative by demonstrating there was no evidence that

Michele was alive. No messages to her family or friends. No credit card activity. No bank loans. No applications for a passport or driver's license. No contact with law enforcement for nearly two decades. It was more than suspicious, but was it proof?

Even if the jury concluded that she was dead, how could the prosecution prove beyond that same standard of reasonable doubt that she had been murdered? That she hadn't died in an accident up in the rugged mountains that made up this part of Colorado, her remains lying at the bottom of some cliff she had failed to climb?

The prosecution would get one shot at Melanson. If they missed, they could never try him again for killing Michele. A detective was even sent to Spain to reinterview the Basque sheepherder who had been a potential suspect. After so long a time, and without Michele's body, it was going to be doubly important to show a jury that they had left no stone unturned.

Young would have had a difficult time explaining why she was so driven. Part of it might have been the closeness in age between herself and Michele, and that they had both come to this same beautiful, rugged country as independent young women looking for adventure. One had found a home, a family, and a career; the other had found death.

Part of it, too, may have been that Michele's was such a sad story. Jackson had told her about the suicide of Maggie Wallace and the note asking that her daughter's body be buried next to her. Young assumed that George Wallace was deceased. There had been no contact with him for more than ten years.

In late 1990, she was talking to a member of the Civil Air Patrol who had been in on the original search, when she learned that Michele had a relative living in Arizona. She called the relative and was surprised to learn that George Wallace was still alive. As a matter of fact, Debbie Fountain and her husband had just left to return home to Florida, where George and his second wife were also living.

Young called Debbie Fountain only to hear from the other woman that she wasn't sure that reopening the case was such a good idea where George was concerned. He had remarried, with a wonderful woman named Melba, but had never really gotten over the deaths of his daughter and first wife. George was near 70 and frail, and Fountain insisted that Young funnel any questions or updates on the case through her, "so I can choose times when he's strong enough."

"Just tell him we're working on the case again," Young said.

After conferring with his investigator and Deputy Jackson, Sheriff Murdie had broached District Attorney Stern with the subject of charging Melanson with Michele Wallace's murder. The prosecutor hadn't said no; in fact, he told Young that if she could find the witnesses after all these years, he might try a bodyless homicide. But, he also cautioned, they were a long way from making a case stick.

A major turning point occurred in early 1991 when Young and Jackson decided to reinventory everything in evidence for the Michele Wallace case. The evidence lists were long, but not very detailed. For instance, they noted the presence of a South Carolina driver's license, but the list didn't specifically state it was Michele's. The investigators were wasting a lot of time when questions arose by having to go and search out individual items; they wanted a master list with complete details.

In the evidence room, they opened one old box and began matching items to the list. Young pulled out a bag with a hairbrush in it. There was a case number on it—Michele's case—written by then- Undersheriff Steve Fry, with a date and the address of Michele's apartment. There was no mention of who it belonged to or where it had come from.

Fry had retired from the department but was still in town, running a sporting goods store. Young called him and asked about the brush. He remembered it well. "I asked for things that only she had used," he said.

Now Kathy Young was really excited. Apparently, when the mass of hair was found in 1979 and sent to the CBI, no one had recalled the hairbrush. Young had noticed that it still contained several long, dark strands of hair.

It would be just one more stone in a field of boulders she had overturned, but she now had a way to prove that the two long braids found on Kebler Pass belonged to Michele Wallace.

Sidetracked by more current cases, Young finally sent the hairbrush and the mass of hair back to the CBI, to their lab in Montrose, on August 1, 1991. Twenty-seven days later, CBI Agent Joe Snyder called. The hair from the brush and the hair found on the pass were a perfect match.

Not long afterward, Young ran into Jennett, the now-former CBI agent. "Mr. Jennett," she said, walking up to the tall, dark-haired criminalist, "I don't know if you remember me, but I used to take classes from you."

Jennett smiled down at the short redheaded woman. "Of course, I remember. What are you up to these days?"

Young explained what she had been doing for the past two years. "I wanted to let you know that we're working the case again," she said. Jennett might be asked to testify, and she was letting him know as a professional courtesy. "And I hope to file charges someday soon."

Jennett nodded. "I always wondered what had happened to that case," he said. "How's it going?"

Young briefed him on what she had. And what she didn't: a body.

Jennett paused and thought a moment, then asked, "You ever hear of the 'pig people'?"

When she shook her head, he went on to explain that a criminalist colleague of his who worked for the Arapahoe County Sheriff's Office, Jack Swanburg, had told him about a new group he was working with. "It's a bunch of scientists and cops who've been burying pigs to see if they can figure out how to find clandestine graves. ... Maybe you ought to give him a call."

"Pig People" was just a nickname, Jennett said. Their real name was NecroSearch International.[9]

---

9   Steve Jackson, *No Stone Unturned* (WildBluePress, May 2015), Kindle Edition

XVII

April 13, 1992

Kathy Young arrived at the penitentiary in Kentucky on what would have been Michele's 43rd birthday. After nearly six years of investigation and preparation, there was one more thing for the intrepid investigator to do: speak to the man who killed Michele at age 25.

There was still hope that Michele's remains could be found before going to trial. Although at first a little skeptical of the group with the morbid-sounding name, she'd met with NecroSearch International in Denver, and they'd agreed to conduct a search for Michele's remains when the snow melted in the Colorado high country.

Not convinced that the NecroSearch team would have any better luck than the thousands of searchers before them, she was nevertheless impressed with their professional and scientific approach. She'd sent them Michele's hair and from studying pine needles and other biological material found in the hair, NecroSearch botanist Vickey Trammell had narrowed the search area. So there was hope.

Whatever happened with the search, the prosecution of Roy Melanson would be going forward. It was under that premise that Sheriff Murdie set up another conference with District Attorney Stern, whose offices were in Montrose, nearly 70 miles west of Gunnison.

The Seventh Judicial District was comprised of six large rural counties, of which Gunnison County was just one. This meant that Stern's resources were stretched thin. Also, the Seventh District wasn't exactly on the cutting edge of homicide trials. In all the years since Michele had disappeared, there had been a handful, all garden variety, quickly solved, and quickly adjudicated.

Stern didn't have the trial experience to handle this one and he knew it. To his credit, he brought his second in command, Wyatt Angelo, an experienced trial attorney, into the conversation.

Still, Stern brought up the usual arguments against prosecuting a body-less homicide—starting with the need to prove that the victim was not only dead, but that she had been murdered. The first was perhaps easier to get past a jury now that seventeen years had elapsed without any word from Michele. However, the second issue—was she murdered?—was more difficult.

Even assuming that the jury agreed that Michele had been murdered, could they prove beyond a reasonable doubt that it was Melanson? His past criminal record, including his rape convictions, would probably not be allowed to be presented to the jury. So how could they prove that he was the killer, rather than Matthews or some unknown assailant who had accosted Michele after Melanson took her car? And finally, what murder charge should they file?

Young and Murdie wanted first-degree murder. At the time of Michele's disappearance, Colorado's death penalty statutes had been struck down as unconstitutional; it had since been reinstated, but they would only be able to charge Melanson as the law applied in 1974. Still, a conviction for first-degree murder would mean life without parole. No woman would ever have to fear him again.

For first-degree murder, the prosecutors would have to prove deliberation—that Melanson had thought out the act of killing Michele before he committed the crime, even if only for a few moments, the time it takes to deliberate. Or would they have to settle for second- degree murder?—that Melanson acted "knowingly," that he knew that what he was doing would likely lead to Michele's death.

Throw all that on top of the fact that the case was nearly two decades old—some of the witnesses were dead; others' memories might be faulty—and they were looking at a difficult conviction at best. At worst, it was a trial they could easily lose.

Wyatt Angelo weighed all this as he listened to Young, Murdie, and Stern. He had been practicing law in Gunnison since 1973, and recalled the disappearance of Michele Wallace. It had been all over the radio and television news, as well as the local newspapers. Other than the media, however, all the information he had up until this point had been by way of the courthouse rumor mill. It was clear then that Melanson was the main suspect, and Angelo had always wondered what happened to the case. Angelo joined the district attorney's office in May 1987, and was promoted to second in line in January 1988. A year later, he had heard about it when Ric Murdie broached the idea of reviving the Wallace case.

Young had with her a photograph of Michele, taken by some unknown person, smiling as she stood with her dog and an unidentified family at some trailhead in the Rocky Mountains. Her hair was in two long, dark braids, just like the hair found on the logging road. This was the young woman they would present to the jury.

Michele and Okie posed for a photograph with an unidentified family while on a backpacking trip shortly before she disappeared. Photo courtesy of Gunnison County District Attorney's Office.

The detective had already done a lot of the homework for the "victimology" Angelo said he would need to try the case. A detailed profile of Michele: her habits, her goals, her relationships with family and friends.

It was apparent to Angelo that he would be able to point out to a jury that Michele had had many reasons to live. She was bright, attractive, engaged with life. She never missed a telephone call to her mother. They might not be allowed to use Mrs. Wallace's suicide in court as evidence of how deep the relationship went, but it was clear that Michele loved and was loved by her family.

She was a budding photographer who would not have blown her first big assignment. Her dearest possession was her camera, and look whose hands it had wound up in, and whose photograph was on the last frame of the roll found in her pawned camera—Roy Melanson. It was a striking piece of circumstantial evidence.

By the time Young had finished answering his questions, Angelo was convinced that, win or lose, they needed to try this case. It was going to be tough; no prosecutor he knew had ever won a body-less homicide trial. Still, when asked by Stern what he thought, he replied, "I'd go with it tomorrow morning."

She wanted to know everything about this man before they met, so she had flown in to Brandenburg, Kentucky, a couple of days earlier to pursue several leads.

One involved two Kentucky inmates who claimed that Melanson had bragged about "disposin' of an unwillin' woman" in the Colorado Mountains "where it's hard to find a body." According to one, Melanson added that he "liked it" when women got "feisty" and he had to get rough with them.

The next lead was a little more unusual. Demonstrating that Melanson had lost none of his charm, he had met a widow through her son, a fellow inmate, and after a brief courtship, talked into her into marriage while he was still in prison.

Young had arranged through Detective Tommy Stiles of the Kentucky State Police to meet another one of the woman's sons— one, Stiles had told her earlier, who wasn't very happy about his mother's marriage.

This son invited Young to their home, where he begged her to speak with his mother. "You tell her about the crimes he's committed," he said. "She won't listen to me. She's head over heels."

Young said she would try. As far as she was concerned, Melanson had victimized enough women, and maybe she could prevent this one from wasting any more of her life on him. Later that day, she met with the new Mrs. Roy Melanson.

She told the woman about the rape cases her husband had already been convicted of, but the woman brushed them off. Roy had told her all about it. "He was wrongfully accused," she said. He had been let go after receiving a life sentence in Texas, he told her, because the authorities there had discovered they had the wrong man.

Young told her it wasn't true. He was let go because his habitual offender conviction was overturned, but nothing the detective said could change the woman's mind.

Young tried a different tack. "You realize that Roy is suspected of beating a man to death in prison?"

The woman smiled as she leaned forward and put her hand on Young's arm. Her husband had told her about that as well. She explained away the alleged beating with a racial slur.

Investigating this case, Young had thought she had encountered just about the worst of human nature. Now, she realized there was always a little room at the bottom of the barrel. At least she no longer felt sorry for the new Mrs. Roy Melanson. She left her and later told the son what had transpired. He shook his head and thanked her for trying.

There was nothing left to do but meet with Melanson himself. Young hadn't planned it so that she would see him on Michele's birthday, but it did seem appropriate. She would have been 43 years old today, the detective thought.

Young was nervous. Not so much for her own safety, although because she was meeting him alone there was that factor, but because she didn't want to take any chances on slipping up. Arrested in Montana, Melanson had fought extradition to Kentucky, but Detective John Carr of the Kentucky State Police had at last brought him back in 1991. He was convicted of burglary with the added sentence enhancement of being a habitual criminal, and sentenced to twenty years. He would be eligible for parole in the year

2002, and if he got out, it would only mean more pain and suffering for some other woman.

This would probably be the one shot a police officer would get at interviewing Melanson about Michele before he "lawyered up," and Young was worried whether she was the right officer for the job. She believed that Melanson hated women, and if her presence was going to wreck any chance of his talking, she was willing to put her ego aside and let a male officer conduct the interview.

Before coming to Kentucky, she had consulted with FBI experts at the agency's behavioral science unit at Quantico. They agreed that Young knew the most about the case and therefore needed to be the one to conduct the interview, she would have to do it without a male officer present or Melanson might ignore her, they counseled.

Detective Stiles, who had taken over the case from Carr, escorted her to the Meade County Courthouse, which adjoined the jail. The conversation would be taped and monitored, and they had arranged certain verbal signals to be used if she felt Melanson was going to attack her. Young soon found herself alone, sitting at a table across from the only door in a small room.

There was a knock on the door. She had been told by Texas Ranger Taylor that Melanson tended to put on weight in prison, but she was surprised when he entered in shackles and handcuffs. He was as big as a bear and had huge hands that seemed disproportionate even for a man as large as he was.

What surprised her more, after he sat down across from her and they started talking, was his demeanor. He was exceptionally polite. "Yes ma'am," he said when they were introduced. "What can I help you with, ma'am?" It continued through their conversation.

They talked in generalities at first. She explained who she was and what case she was working on. He asked if the old Sheriff, Claude Porterfield, was still in office. Melanson considered himself quite an artist, and he had given one of the paintings he'd done in the Gunnison County Jail to the Sheriff back in 1974.

Melanson's tone was reassuring. He didn't try to come on to her, or give her the once-over with his eyes she had expected. He was every bit a gentleman.

She felt herself relaxing. Then suddenly, the hair on the back of her neck stood on end and she felt a chill. *Oh my God,* she thought to herself, *this is how he does it!* The nice guy. Polite. Yes, ma'am. No, ma'am. ... Until his victim relaxed.

Young shook off her antipathy as if waking up from a nap. She knew who he was and what he was, and yet she had felt herself lulled by his pleasant manners. She was glad Stiles was just outside the room. "I'm letting you know that I'm not giving up on this case," she said firmly. "This case will go to a conclusion, and you're the main suspect. There is no one else but you."

For the first time, Melanson dropped the veneer, just slightly. He continued to address her politely, but there was now an edge to his voice when he declared, "You people were wasting your time back then, and you're wasting your time now."

Young got to Melanson again by showing him a photograph of Michele's hair. He stopped what he was saying in mid-sentence and looked stunned. His mouth twitched. Then he quickly changed the subject.

Their conversation only lasted about twenty minutes before Melanson abruptly ended it. If she tried to talk to him again, he said, he would want a lawyer present.

Young had gained nothing that could be used as evidence in court, nor any hints about what he had done with Michele's body. It wasn't a complete waste, however. She had a keener insight into Melanson's psyche, and she had learned that he could be rattled by his victim.

Later as she turned in for the night, Young murmured, "Happy Birthday, Michele. We're still working on it." She flew back to Colorado the next day, more determined than ever to take this to trial. Her boss agreed, and on April 22nd, Roy Melanson was served in his cell with an arrest warrant for murder.

A heated discussion followed between Sheriff Murdie and Stern, who had wanted to delay serving the warrant. The sheriff and Young had agreed though, no more stalling.

Stern wasn't the person most upset about the warrant. That fell to Melanson. He soon wrote a letter to Gunnison County District Judge Tom Goldsmith.

Melanson demanded that Kathy Young be removed from the case. She was prejudiced against him, he claimed. She had had him hauled out of prison in shackles and handcuffs and dragged down to the courthouse to grill him. No other prisoner was ever treated so rudely, he claimed.

Besides, contended Melanson, who after spending most of his adult life in prison had become what he considered quite the jailhouse lawyer, the state had no case. "There's no *corpus delicti*," he pointed out. No body.

Angelo said he was willing to prosecute the case regardless. "We'll do the best we can," he told Young. "If Melanson walks away from Michele's murder, at least we'll know we tried." Young was willing to try just about anything to succeed. When she got a call from NecroSearch early that summer, Swanburg, the president said, if she was still interested, the group would send a search team in August.

Why not, Young thought to herself. She didn't hold out much hope, but if they wanted to try, she was willing to let them.

XVIII

August 23, 1994

The murder trial of Roy Melanson began without his presence because he refused to attend. Instead, he sat in his jail cell listening over an audio system created just for him. The telephone was provided in case he wanted to confer with his attorneys.

Melanson had called the local newspapers to explain his reasons. He was innocent, he contended, but he also wasn't going to participate as long as he was forced to wear a "shock belt," otherwise known as a custody control device. One wrong move to escape or otherwise cause trouble, and a deputy sheriff in the courtroom could press a button and send 50,000 volts of electricity for 8 seconds into the wearer.

Sheriff Murdie had insisted on Melanson wearing the belt for the safety of those attending the trial. Melanson claimed the belt was "degrading. ... It's intended for nothing but pain and suffering." Melanson had taken his complaints to the judge. In documents filed for him by his lawyer, he contended that the Sheriff was "motivated by malice, vindictiveness, intolerance, and prejudice." The authorities, he added, "were seeking to vindicate their otherwise absolute power over me while I am under their control."

The sheriff's office had assured Melanson and the court that he would be given loose-fitting civilian clothes to wear during his trial, which would disguise the bulky contraption from the jury. It wasn't good enough for Melanson. Defense lawyer Harvey Pelefsky told the press that there was another reason Melanson was boycotting his trial: His client was upset that Michele's remains would be presented to the jury.

Thanks to the extraordinary efforts of NecroSearch International there was no need to attempt to prosecute Roy Melanson for the murder of Michele Wallace with no, as he was fond of saying, *"corpus delicti."*

In August 1992, on a steep slope below an old logging road on Kebler Pass, a gold filling in a molar gleaming in the sun had led NecroSearch naturalist Cecilia Travis to a skull. Further searching led the team to the rest of the remains wedged against a tree a few feet farther up the hill.

NecroSearch member Diane France, a forensic anthropologist by trade, determined that based on the final resting place of the remains, she believed that the body had been thrown from the road above. A short time later, a forensic odontologist determined from dental records that the skull definitively belonged to Michele Wallace.

Over the course of Roy Melanson's trial, the prosecution planned to call thirty-nine witnesses, including the Pueblo cops and FBI agents originally involved in the investigation. They would present fifty-five exhibits, such as Michele Wallace's driver's license, car registration and an unused bus ticket found on Melanson in 1974. They would show the photograph taken from Michele's pawned camera depicting Melanson on a couch and call the teenager, now a woman, to the stand to talk about when it was taken.

However, the most stunning exhibits, those that most troubled Melanson, were Michele's remains. That had become clear at a pre-trial hearing six months after they were found.

Thanks to NecroSearch, the prosecutors had proof that Michele was dead, although they still couldn't prove how she died. France's examination of the bones had turned up no new clues. The trial was anything but a shoo-in. Not that it was unexpected, but they weren't going to be allowed to bring in testimony about Melanson's previous rape convictions or current incarceration.

The legal reasoning for the exclusion of "prior bad acts" evidence is that a defendant shouldn't be held accountable for past offenses, and the jury should only consider the present charge. However, the ruling meant the defense attorneys could raise questions about what motive their client would have had to kill Michele.

The prosecutors would have to bite their tongues rather than reply that the answer was "Because he rapes women and likes it when they get feisty and he has to get rough with them." Meanwhile, any criminal acts or other foibles of the prosecution witnesses would be fair game for the defense attorneys.

The only clue the jury would get that Melanson was something other than a 56-year-old drifter was a weak explanation of how he came to know prosecution witnesses John Paul Steele and Jack Hassig. The prosecutors were going to be allowed to introduce into evidence the fact that Melanson had been in the Gunnison County Jail on forgery charges in 1974-75 but had been acquitted.

On the day of the hearing, Melanson was led into the courtroom in handcuffs and shackles and wearing a jail jumpsuit. He glanced at a stand in the middle of the courtroom, on which something square had been placed beneath a black cloth.

As Argali outlined the government's case, he had moved up to the stand. "Your honor," the prosecutor said, "People's Exhibit ..." and removed the black cloth.

The cloth, which Argali had purposely made sure was black for mourning, had covered a square glass case.

Mounted inside the case on a glass rod was the skull of Michele Wallace. At all previous hearings, Melanson had hardly done more than look bored. This time, he blanched, and his right hand, which had been resting on the table, began to shake as he leaned back in his chair to look at Young, who was sitting to his left at the prosecution table.

Surely his lawyers told him that we'd found her remains, Young had thought as she returned the look, but this seemed to have taken him by surprise. Angelo had told her to watch for Melanson's reaction; maybe it could be used in court. She recalled how he had behaved in Kentucky when shown the photograph of Michele's hair. This had hit him even harder.

As he caught her eye, he had nodded, and ever after Young would wonder if the expression on his face was a smirk, a grimace, or an acknowledgment that she had him beat. *Gotcha,* she had thought, *that will teach you to underestimate the police.*

When Melanson refused to attend the actual trial, the prosecution team believed the presence of the remains had more to do with Melanson's absence than anything else. Those remains were in the courtroom within three rectangular boxes of various sizes and covered by black cloth, awaiting the right moment for their display.

Angelo opened for the prosecution, outlining the case and the various characters who would be introduced, such as Chuck Matthews, Sally Burton, and Michele's father, George. He talked about how Melanson, Matthews, and Michele Wallace had met, and noted the statements the defendant made to inmates in Gunnison and Kentucky, remarks made about a shallow grave and knocking out the victim's teeth. "He said he had to dispose of an 'unwilling girl' in Colorado."

The prosecutor paused, then, looking into the eyes of the jurors, he concluded his opening: "That sexually unwilling girl was found a year ago this month. She was found on Kebler Pass, where Roy Melanson went with Chuck Matthews to look for a nonexistent cabin. She was murdered on or about August thirtieth, when she fell into the hands of Roy Melanson."

When Angelo finished, attorney Natalie Frei opened for the defense. She was a young, pretty public defender appointed to the case at the taxpayers' expense. She had worried the prosecution team at early hearings with what they felt was her overly solicitous manner around Melanson, placing herself, they felt, at risk of being taken hostage.

Addressing the jury, Frei said the evidence would demonstrate that Melanson was a thief but nothing more. "He stole Michele's car. He stole her camping gear. He stole her camera. That's what the evidence in this case will show. ... What it doesn't show is that he murdered her."

When Frei took her seat, Judge Richard Brown instructed the prosecution to call its first witness. Angelo rose and announced, "The People call George Wallace."

Young had finally contacted George Wallace after the remains were found. Up until that point, she had been going through his relatives. She still felt she had to write to Wallace directly, and told him that, if he wanted, she would be glad to hear from him personally.

She wrote that as a person and a police officer, she wanted to let him know that the door was open. "I'll answer any questions I can," she said. If she didn't hear from him, she would construe that to mean that he was satisfied with the current arrangement.

A month later, she got a phone call from George, and he very much wanted to talk. Soon they were speaking often by telephone. He told her a lot about Michele—the little things that rounded out her personality—and Young found herself wishing they had begun communicating sooner.

George Wallace had remarried, but he had never gotten over the loss of his daughter and his first wife, often breaking into tears as he recalled old memories for Young. Receiving the news from the search had been bittersweet in more ways than one, for it came at the same time he had learned that his second wife, Melba, had cancer. It only deepened his hatred for Roy Melanson—something bad seemed to happen whenever he heard that name.

It had eaten at him that the man who he knew had killed his daughter and caused the death of his first wife went unpunished. It had looked as though he might get away with it forever until Kathy Young had come along, and then this wonderful group of people, NecroSearch, who found his daughter's remains.

Wallace had shown a great deal of interest in the concept behind NecroSearch. He would always be grateful to them and Young, who he regarded as something of a miracle worker. There was still a trial to get through. Only when it was over, one way or another, would he at last fulfill his promise to Maggie Wallace. He would be able to bury their daughter next to her.

The night before the trial, Young and Angelo met George Wallace at the Gunnison airport. Angelo had work to do, so Young drove George to the motel where he would spend the night. As they parted, the stocky, white-haired old man handed the young detective a large envelope and asked her not to open it until she was alone. It would be too emotional for him, he said.

When she opened the envelope later, Young found a black-and- white photograph inside. It was grainy and highly contrasted, and it appeared to have been taken in winter, when the leaves had fallen from the thin, dark trees of a park. The slender silhouette of a young woman stood in a clearing, turning toward a bright light coming up over a hill in the background.

Young turned the photograph over. On the back, there was a message, as if written by Michele:

To Kathy Young,

Though I have been gone for so long, I am glad you remembered me!

Thank you, "Mush," Michele Wallace.

Below that:

This was written by my appreciative father for me. My mother will be so happy when I am at her side. May God bless you and your family. My picture is titled, "Coming Home."

The next morning Wallace found out that Melanson wasn't going to attend the trial. He exploded and told Angelo that he wasn't going to show up either.

"I want to see that bastard," he yelled. "That son of a bitch. I want to look him square in the eye." He had waited all these years to face Melanson and accuse him to his face. Now, he would be robbed of even that satisfaction.

The disappearance of his daughter and the death of his first wife had nearly killed him twenty years ago. All the joy had gone out of his life, and he let his restaurant go downhill. He didn't care. His weight had dropped from 240 pounds to 175 pounds, which under other circumstances would have been a good thing. But it wasn't healthy. He was just wasting away.

Wallace had never touched alcohol. He had always believed that drinking was the downfall of many a restaurant/bar owner. Yet, a year after the two women left him alone, he was seriously considering drowning all his sorrows in a bottle.

Then he was saved by love. George had sold the restaurant and was going through the motions for a couple of days more before walking away for good when a middle-aged woman came in for dinner. She was alone, and they got to chatting. She said her name was Melba. She had been recently widowed after thirty years of marriage.

Melba was so easy to talk to. In minutes it seemed as though they were old friends. After a while, she noticed a photograph of Michele he had on the wall behind the cash register.

"That's my daughter," he had said when he noticed her gaze. He told her the tragic story, not caring that he cried in front of this woman he hardly knew. She then asked for the photograph and, from that day on, carried it in her purse as though Michele had been her daughter, too.

Melba and George were both lonely and needed someone. It wasn't long before he proposed and they were married. A few years later, they had moved to St. Petersburg, Florida, where they began a new life and lived happily ever since. She was the most understanding woman he had ever met. She wasn't jealous of the other women who had been part of her new husband's life and for whom he still grieved.

In fact, she worked to keep the memory of Maggie and Michele alive in her home. She was there also to hold him when some new piece of news came out of Colorado regarding his missing daughter. She told him it was okay to cry, that you never lose the feelings you have for someone you loved.

"I am very lucky," George Wallace had told Kathy Young after they began talking. "I found love twice in my life."

They had been married nearly nineteen years. Good years. But that, too, was coming to an end. Melba was very sick with cancer, and he was going to lose her.

Finding Michele after so long had seemed like a miracle. He couldn't say enough good things about NecroSearch. Before they found Michele's remains, he had been warned through his relatives that the prosecutors thought that charging Melanson was risky. Wallace felt that they should try him anyway—better to lose than not make the attempt.

The prosecutors were now a whole lot more optimistic since Michele had been found. Wallace had been a little taken aback by the site of her skull in the glass case, but he had been happy to hear how it shook up Melanson at the pretrial hearing. *Anything to get that bastard,* he thought. It was too bad Melanson couldn't get the death penalty. Thanks to Young and NecroSearch, there was a good chance he would never get out of prison again.

Wallace had looked forward to seeing that knowledge in Melanson's eyes, but now they were telling him that his daughter's killer didn't have to face his accusers. It was as if he was sitting back there in some little room, laughing at them all again. Wallace wasn't even going to be able to stay for the whole trial; there weren't too many more days left for Melba, and he needed to be near her.

Angelo tried to settle his witness down. They were both from the same area of Chicago originally, so the prosecutor talked about the old neighborhood and about Michele's childhood there before bringing up the subject of Wallace's testimony again.

"George," Angelo said at last, "we have the case whether he comes or not."

But Wallace was still too angry. "I want to see that son of a bitch in front of me," he demanded.

Angelo got District Attorney Stern on the telephone. "I'll tell you why you should appear," Stern said to Wallace. "We can put that man away without him being there. And if we do, he'll never hurt another woman like Michele again."

It was that thought that finally swayed George Wallace. Maybe the deaths of Michele and Maggie wouldn't be in vain if a monster like Melanson never saw another day of freedom. He didn't like it, but he said he would take the stand and testify against a man who didn't have the balls to face him in court.

Wallace entered the courtroom and strode up to the area in front of the judge, where he raised his right hand and swore to tell the truth. George Wallace was 54 when Michele disappeared; he was 73 now and angry. He had also been told that he wouldn't be allowed to talk about Maggie's suicide. It might infringe on the bastard's rights.

Tears began to roll down his cheeks when he was asked the name of his first wife. "Maggie Wallace," he said. They continued to fall as the questions dragged up the past, one painful memory at a time. "How long?" Angelo asked.

"Thirty-four years."

"Children?"

"Two. One boy and one girl." The boy, he said, was named George Junior. The girl was Michele.

In the summer of 1974, he and his wife were living in Chicago, running a successful Italian restaurant, he said. His daughter had moved to Gunnison "to photograph Colorado."

"That summer were you all in good health?"

"Excellent," Wallace answered. "Perfect."

"When Michele was away from home did she maintain contact?" "Always," her father replied. "At least weekly, in between all her activities."

"Who made the calls?"

"My wife and Michele, mostly. One or the other was always calling."

"If I asked you to describe Michele's personality traits, what would you say?" Angelo asked.

"She was an adventurous girl," Wallace replied, but he was then overwhelmed by the image of his lively daughter. "Sorry..." he stammered. Some members of the jury were also dabbing at their eyes.

Wallace talked about his daughter's plans for the future, and about her best friend, Okie. "Would Michele have done anything to protect Okie from harm?" Angelo asked.

"Definitely," Wallace nodded.

"Would she have separated herself from Okie to protect him?" "Depending on the situation," Wallace agreed. "If it was to protect him from harm, I guess she would have."

George Wallace was told he could step down. "Sorry, I was such a ..." he began but couldn't finish.

The prosecution then called Chuck Matthews to the stand. The years and the drinking had been hard on the Army veteran and ranch hand; his face was weathered and his eyes bloodshot. He had married and divorced five women. He gladly answered the call to testify at Melanson's trial, however, making the long bus ride from, appropriately, Truth or Consequences, New Mexico. He might be a drunk, but he wasn't the kind of man who could abide some guy hurting a woman—he had never so much as slapped one of his ex-wives. There was also another score to settle between him and Melanson.

Matthews realized that when he was driving down all those isolated logging roads at his companion's insistence, he was being set up for murder. In particular, he had recalled the time he handed the rifle to Melanson and then turned his back. "Hell, he probably woulda' shot me," Matthews had told Young, "if he'd a' thought my car would get him to Pueblo."

Neither the prosecution nor Matthews attempted to hide from the jury that he was an alcoholic who had never quite readjusted after the Vietnam War. His memory was a little fuzzy on some of the chronology and place names from his trek with Melanson. Matthews's candor often provided a little levity to the proceedings, such as when on cross-examination Pelefsky kept hammering at his drinking. "Isn't it true that you were a fixture at every bar in the area?" the defense attorney had asked.

"Well, yeah," Matthews said with a nod and a good-natured smile, "I didn't want to be prejudiced." The defense attorneys were the only ones in the courtroom not to laugh.

Matthews was serious, however, when he discussed his adventure with Roy Melanson. He said he "got along great" with the German shepherd. He was just sorry that he had let the girl drive off alone with his drinking partner.

One of the items Melanson feared was revealed when the first rectangular object, the smallest of the three, was uncovered while the wife of the man Kolz, who had discovered Michele's hair in 1979, and had since died, took the stand. Beneath the cloth was a lovely wooden box with a glass cover, and inside, laid out on light-blue velvet, was the hair.

The prosecution phase of the trial was drawing to a close—just a couple of witnesses left—when Kathy Young took the stand. She was there mostly to tie the rest of it together as the one person who saw the whole picture, but without her, there would have been no case.

Young talked a lot about the evidence, noting such important facts as Melanson feeling comfortable enough to pawn Michele's equipment using his own name, and driving more than a thousand miles in her car bearing South Carolina plates. Using a large map, Young traced Melanson's travels from Gunnison to Pueblo to Kansas to Iowa to Oklahoma to Texas and back to Colorado.

Part of her investigation had been to run down other leads and look at other suspects, including Chuck Matthews, she said. All of the other leads had either not panned out, or they came back to point at the man who was noticeably absent from his seat at the defense table.

Young described how she and Scott Jackson had found the brush with the hair on it, and thought to send it to the CBI, along with the mass of hair the jury could see in front of it. "It came back a match for Michele Wallace," she said.

The hair had led her to NecroSearch, she said, then described her part in the finding and recovery of Michele Wallace's remains. Most of that information, however, she left for Cecilia Travis and, particularly, Diane France.

It felt good to be finally telling a jury, representatives of her community, what had happened all those years ago. She knew from her investigation that a lot of people had never forgotten the name of Michele Wallace and how her disappearance had taken some measure of innocence from their beautiful part of the country.

Cecilia Travis was called to the stand. The petite naturalist matter-of-factly talked about the purpose of NecroSearch and how she came to be crawling around in the vegetation on Kebler Pass.

She described spotting the "mushroom" that had turned out to be the skull of Michele Wallace. As she spoke, Angelo walked over to the second of the rectangular boxes and removed the black cloth. Inside its glass case was the object of Travis' testimony, the reminder of Michele that had so greatly disturbed Roy Melanson.

The jury stared at the case and its contents in fascination. There before them was the reality of Michele's fate. Not some theory proposed by attorneys, but white bone and a gold filling. The actual skull of Michele Wallace.

Finally, the stage was set for Diane France. By the time she showed up at the Gunnison County Courthouse for Roy Melanson's trial, it seemed to France that every time she turned around, there was a new case involving the murder of a 20-something-year-old woman. At least with Michele Wallace, there was some consolation in being able to give some closure to the family, as well as to a dedicated cop like Kathy Young.

Perhaps, France hoped, she would find some peace in that, too. She had a few butterflies as she entered the courtroom to take the stand. She had met with the prosecution team the night before and felt confident that she was prepared to answer any questions that might come up. Angelo had told her only to speak to what she knew. She knew that no one else in that courtroom was better able to talk about forensic anthropology and the recovery of Michele Wallace's remains than she was.

As discussed the night before, Angelo led her through a series of questions about how NecroSearch went about setting up the search scene, how Michele's skull was discovered, and the procedures that followed.

Finally, the last black cloth was removed from the third rectangular object. It was a wooden box about 5 feet long, the insides of which were lined with light-blue velvet. Beneath the glass cover, every bone that had been found, except the skull, had been sewn into its anatomically correct position. Other items, such as the pieces of bra and the boot with the foot bones had also been included. The jury now had the hair, skull, and recovered bones of Michele Wallace in full view.

None of the witnesses at this trial was able to say how Michele had died; too much time had passed. But France could describe the circumstances surrounding the deposition of Michele's body based on what was found at the scene. In her expert opinion, she said, the original site of deposition was the base of the tree, 25 feet below the road.

At different points in her testimony, Angelo handed her photographs from the scene to describe before passing them on to the jury. She hadn't seen these particular photographs, so she did her best on short notice to describe what the jury would see.

"This is the overall scene," she said of one. "This is a bra clasp ... this shows bits of a bra ... that's the zipper to a pair of jeans ... that's a femur ... this is her vertebra."

Angelo handed her one photograph that showed her bending over from behind, but for the life of her, she didn't know what it was trying to depict. "And what do we see here, Dr. France?" Angelo asked.

France hesitated, and then told the truth. "There's nothing in here but my rear end." This time even the defense lawyers joined the rest of the courtroom in laughter.

France's testimony lasted less than an hour and when it was over, she felt enormous relief. And, she thought as she left the courtroom, it felt good to have spoken for Michele Wallace.

Before the prosecution ended its case, and against the protests of the defense attorneys, the jury was taken to the site where Michele Wallace's remains were found. The prosecutors had persuaded the judge that it was important for the jurors to see for themselves the site that Young, Travis, and France had described.

On the logging road above the site, with the court reporter perched on a little stool in the middle of the road with her equipment, the judge gave the jury a brief description of what was found. Young then led a tour—the jurors had been told to dress for hiking this day—where she pointed at various spots. "This is where the cranium was discovered. ... This is the base of the tree where most of the bones were discovered."

After their return to the courtroom, the defense's case was short. The attorneys presented only four witnesses, recalling former sheriff Claude Porterfield and former undersheriff Fry. Both were questioned about the quality of the search at the time of Michele's disappearance, and whether leads regarding other suspects had been followed.

Throughout the prosecution witnesses' testimony, the telephone on the defense table had remained silent. Then one day, it rang loudly. The sudden intrusion jarred everybody nearly out of their seats, and Pelefsky quickly grabbed it and spoke quietly into the mouthpiece.

It turned out that Melanson had seen Sally Burton and her sisters in the parking lot from his jail cell. Recognizing Sally after all those years, he now wanted to talk to her. That wasn't going to happen, but she was called by his attorneys to testify.

The telephone remained quiet while she described her relationship with Melanson. He never raped her, she said, but she also knew that she had no choice but to comply with his demands for sex. She recalled how quickly he could move, and the implied threats when she gave any indication of trying to leave the cabin. She still remembered the little red car he used to drive her and her sisters around Pueblo.

In the end, it was a toss-up whether Burton's testimony had been more beneficial to the defense or the prosecution. Although he had never attacked her, this was a man who had kept a 14-year-old girl a virtual prisoner in a cabin for a week.

At last the moment had come for closing arguments. Angelo began by noting to the jury that in their instructions from the court they had been told to "feel free to apply their life experiences" while deliberating. "This is not a laboratory." Reasonable doubt was not the absence of doubt, but "doubt based upon reason and common sense."

The evidence in the case, Angelo concluded, pointed squarely at Roy Melanson as the man who killed Michele Wallace, "and that he planned to do so. ... I trust that you will return with a verdict of first-degree murder for the death of Michele Wallace."

Pelefsky began his closing arguments by referring to the movie *Twelve Angry Men.* By "all appearances ... it appeared that the defendant was guilty," the attorney said. But one man, played by Henry Fonda, had insisted that his fellow jurors look more closely at the government's case, and in the end, the defendant was acquitted. He suggested that the jury sift through the evidence "much as NecroSearch sifted through the dirt, and let's look and see if there was reasonable doubt."

The case was a puzzle, and if the pieces fit together, "then convict him; convict him of first-degree murder if that's the picture you get. But if it's an obscure picture, an incomplete picture ... then there is reasonable doubt and you must acquit."

"Roy Melanson was a drifter," Pelefsky conceded. "A petty thief. A con artist who used people and lived from day to day. ... He moved around and got people to do things for him. ... It was how Roy Melanson lived. Whether you approve or don't, he used his charm to use people. ... But being a con artist, being a petty thief, being someone who uses people does not a murderer make."

In his rebuttal, Angelo noted, "Mr. Pelefsky suggested that motive is important. I'll give two. If the crime was theft, you don't leave someone to point the finger at you. If the crime was rape, same thing."

Angelo urged the jury to take special notice of People's Exhibit 47, the zipper found by NecroSearch. The zipper clasp was at the top, but the other side was gone. "What's chilling is if you look down the front of the zipper where the other side should be... there's a broken tooth ripped from the other side of her Levi's.... That's your motive."

Angelo concluded by turning around Pelefsky's remarks about justice and Roy Melanson. "My request to you is that you give Michele Wallace her justice. It is nineteen years, almost to the day, that she died. She is entitled to some."

The jury thought so, too. On September 1, after just 51/2 hours of deliberation, but nearly two decades in coming, they returned with a verdict of murder in the first degree.

Following the trial, the jurors met with Kathy Young. They were all impressed by the sheer amount of circumstantial evidence, and each seemed to have picked up on different aspects of the trial. Some were convinced that Melanson's use of his own name to pawn Michele's equipment proved he knew she was dead. They all believed Steele's account of his long-ago conversation with Melanson.

One woman said that not only did she believe every word Matthews said, she "wanted to take him home and feed him." Another juror asked if they had staged the emotions of George Wallace. When she denied it, he shook his head and said, "I thought it was too emotional not to believe."

The jurors agreed that Angelo had done a magnificent job of tying together a complex case. The defense, however, particularly in its closing, acted as if they didn't believe in their client's innocence and were "grasping at straws."

The jurors each l seemed to have one small thing they had picked out. For some, it was the way Melanson had driven around in Michele's car so brazenly, knowing there was no one to report it stolen. One man thought it was incriminating to have found Okie's leash in the car when Melanson had claimed he last saw the dog tied up outside the bar where he left Michele. A woman thought Michele would have had the insurance card on her person unless it had been taken.

However, they all reported having been most affected by the site where her remains were found. For some, it was the remoteness; for others, it matched Matthews's description of his travels with Melanson: the steep slope, the thick vegetation ...

It all fit so well with the testimony of Diane France, who had related her findings in such amazing but understandable detail to what they saw at the site. Would they have convicted Melanson without Michele's remains? The jurors said, there was no ignoring the bones of Michele Wallace. "It made her real," said one juror.

That afternoon, Melanson was brought into the courtroom he had sought to avoid. Judge Brown sentenced him to life in prison, to run consecutive to his Kentucky sentence. In pronouncing judgment, Brown read from the U.S. Constitution and the Declaration of Independence, as Melanson stood sullen and brooding, noting that the defendant had deprived Michele Wallace of her "life, liberty and pursuit of happiness."

"Quite frankly, you are nothing more than a big mouth and a big braggart with an empty mind and no conscience," the judge said. "People have a right to be free, Mr. Melanson. People have a right to be free from people like you. You're a waste of humanity."

Melanson showed no reaction. He just sat and stared straight ahead as if bored.

It was a bright, warm end-of-the-summer day when the prosecutors, Sheriff Murdie, and Young at last left the courtroom. There wasn't a cloud in the sky outside, but just as they stepped out the door, there was an enormous clap of thunder.

"I guess someone else approves," Kathy Young said, and they all laughed.[10]

---

10   Steve Jackson, *No Stone Unturned* (WildBluePress, May 2015), Kindle Edition

XIX

April 13, 1994

Donna Campeglia looked around at those gathered at the Woodland Cemetery in Riverside, Illinois. On what would have been her 45th birthday, the ashes of Michele Wallace were being buried in her mother's grave and more than 150 people had gathered for the Mass and memorial service she'd arranged.

Contacting the media who jumped on the heart-wrenching story, she'd wanted everyone who knew Michele or had wondered about her disappearance all those years ago to know that she'd been found, her killer tried and convicted, and that she was now coming home. Amazed by the size of the crowd, she recognized old friends and their parents from high school and the neighborhood, teachers and former co-workers.

Also present was Michele's father, George Sr., brother, George Jr., and the woman who she believed had made this final homecoming possible, Kathy Young. She'd met Kathy the day before and given her a whirlwind tour of Chicago and presented her with a plaque, thanking her for her persistence and dedication.

Life had never been the same after Michele's disappearance and death. A fear factor had entered her formerly happy-go-lucky life. It wasn't just that she wouldn't go alone to walk dogs in the woods, or was always looking over her shoulder, wondering if some man was about to grab her; she was skeptical of anyone she met, she didn't trust people. After all, Melanson had come off as just a charming, smooth-talking man when really he was just an evil liar and murderer.

Donna tried not to think much about Melanson. She didn't like looking at photographs of him. She was afraid his evil would somehow permeate her being. But she'd recently seen a photograph of him taken from a prison in Kentucky where he'd been interviewed by one of the newspapers prior to the memorial service. He admitted to the journalist that he'd stolen Michele's car and other belongings, but denied killing her. *"I've always wondered what really happened to her,"* he was quoted. *"I am not a monster."*

Really? she thought when she read that statement. *Then what should we call a person who beats and molests women, eventually killing them, so that he can steal their belongings and go off on his merry way?*

After Michele's murder she'd become fascinated with watching crime shows. She thought she might see or hear something that would help her solve Michele's disappearance and murder. Then it was just a morbid fascination with the amount of violent crime and murder that permeated society; Melanson was the poster boy for all of that, the monster who lurked in the shadows of her mind.

Yet, neither the years nor the skepticism nor the television crime shows, could dissipate the love she still had for her friend or the memories. Indeed, for years she'd "protected" her mind from reality by "pretending" that Michele had tumbled down a mountainside, struck her head and got amnesia. It meant she was still out there somewhere, not knowing who she was but alive … and maybe someday would come home again.

Of course, when Michele's remains were found, even that fantasy was dashed. But her memories remained, reinforced by the "arty" photographs that Michele had taken of her when they were young and were hanging on the walls of her home, daily reminders of her friend. She'd also kept every letter she'd ever received in a box.

Budding photograph Michele Wallace took this photograph of her best friend Donna Campeglia. It still hangs on a wall in Campeglia's home in Illinois. Photo by Michele Wallace.

When she heard that Michele's remains had been cremated, she'd arranged for the Mass and services, knowing that George Sr. was overwhelmed with yet another tragedy in his life.

The day the Gunnison coroner called George Wallace to ask where to send the ashes, the old man had just minutes before returned home from the hospital and the bedside of his wife, Melba. She had died that afternoon.

Michele's remains arrived in Florida where he'd moved, the same day that he picked up Melba's ashes. It was almost more than one man could bear, and still he had another dilemma to face.

When he was married to Maggie, George had reserved a place for the two of them, side by side in Woodlawn Cemetery. He had never dreamed he would have to bury two wives and a daughter before he, too, passed on. But if he buried Melba next to Maggie, there wouldn't be any more space available in the original plot, and Maggie had asked to have her daughter buried next to her. Nor did he want to be separated in death, as he was in life, from the three women he loved.

Heartsick and unsure of what to do, George wrestled with the problem until he discovered that Illinois law allowed one body and the cremated remains of a second person to be buried in the same grave. Michele and her mother would at last be reunited, and George would be buried with Melba's ashes, next to the grave of his beloved first wife and daughter.

George had Kathy Young, who sat next to him at the ceremony, and the wonderful people at NecroSearch to thank for bringing Michele back to her mother. And her best friend, Donna Campeglia, who saw that "Mush" was surrounded by people who had loved her. She'd never been forgotten, and now they could all find peace and let her go.

Just like in the photograph he treasured and given to Young, Michele was turning toward the light; she was going home.[11]

---

11 Tragedy would continue to follow the Wallace family. In January 2006, two young thugs entered the St. Petersburg home of George Wallace, eighty-five-years old and confined to a wheelchair. They put a comforter over his head and beat him unconscious then ransacked his home and took his car. Wallace died in the hospital eight hours later.
The killers, Stephen Sterling, 22, and Eugene Wesley, 17, were eventually arrested. Two years later, Wesley testified against Sterling and pleaded guilty to second-degree murder; he was sentenced to 25 years. Sterling was convicted of first degree murder and sentenced to life without parole.

XX

November 5, 2009

The barely restrained excitement in the woman's voice on the other end of the line made Napa police detective Don Winegar sit up. "We got a hit," she said. "It's for a convicted murderer named Roy Melanson. He's incarcerated in Colorado."

Winegar couldn't believe what he was hearing from Michelle Terra, a criminalist who worked for the California Department of Justice DNA laboratory. After 35 years, there was a name for the stranger sitting at the end of bar, smoking a cigarette, at Fagiani's Cocktail Lounge on the night of July 10, 1974.

Roy Melanson. Didn't ring a bell, but Winegar, who knew every name and detail having to do with the case, didn't care. *We got a hit!*

The 52-year-old detective had been working on the cold case homicide since 2006; the last in a line of investigators assigned or inclined to look into the murder of Anita Andrews. He'd picked up the case after he and Detective Todd Shulman solved another homicide through hard work and the relatively new crime-fighting tool, for Napa anyway, of DNA comparison analysis.

The result of the other case meant life without parole Eric Copple, a 26-year-old man who had stabbed two young women to death in November 2004. Based on the success of

DNA evidence used to convict Copple, chief of detectives Sgt. Tim Cantillon had asked Winegar and Shulman to look at other cold cases that might be solved through DNA.

The science of comparing *Deoxyribonucleic acid,* a molecule found in all living organisms, and with humans can be used to match blood, semen, skin, saliva and hair found at a crime scene, to that of a suspect was first used to convict a killer in 1988. Since then the science had slowly gained widespread acceptance in courtrooms. But even twenty years after that first conviction, the process was expensive and slow, especially in light of the sheer number of cases that constantly inundated understaffed and underfunded crime laboratories, such as at the California Department of Justice.

Shulman took the case of Doreen Heskett, a five-year-old girl who had gone missing on March 3, 1963, and whose skeletal remains had been discovered in a field nine months later. Winegar chose the Anita Andrews homicide.

The science of DNA comparison was interesting to Winegar, who early in his law enforcement career had worked as at the Napa County Sheriff's Office as a patrol officer and deputy coroner investigating causes of death. But he'd harbored few illusions that three years later it would put him on the doorstep of cracking one of the county's oldest unsolved cases.

Hired by the Napa Police Department in 1987 and a detective since the late 1990s, Winegar was well aware of the local legend behind the still-closed and shuttered Fagiani's Cocktail Lounge in downtown Napa. Just about anybody who'd ever spent any time in Napa, especially in law enforcement, knew about the murder of Anita Andrews. Anita's sister, Muriel Fagiani, was a well-known gadfly at city council meetings, sticking up for long-time residents as "progress" threatened the Napa way of life, but also reminding anybody who'd listen that her sister's killer was still a mystery.

It seemed like every five years or so, the media would trot out the story and different detectives who worked on the case would be interviewed though there was never much new to add. Like most small cities, Napa didn't have a cold case homicide unit dedicated to just old unsolved cases. If a detective worked on a cold case, it was in addition to their regular full caseloads, and because detectives were transferred in and out of investigations every few years, it was hard to put much time or effort into solving one.

Winegar was no different. He had a full caseload and could only work on the Andrews murder in fits and starts when time allowed.

Initially he began looking at the evidence kept in the Records and Property Divisions, which consisted of three binders with reports, and a number of boxes containing the physical evidence, miraculously including three boxes of beer bottles that had not been thrown away.

At first he viewed the reports in the binders as historical documents to be read and put in some sort of order. As he began creating binders of his own, such as one in which he listed every name and the facts associated with those names, he was cognizant of the fact that what happened the night of July 10, 1974 wasn't only a murder, but also a sexual assault and a robbery, both of which might be important for establishing motive if a suspect was identified.

He read reports generated by other detectives over the years, particularly the first two assigned to the case, Robert Jarecki and John Bailey. He noted the good old-fashioned gumshoe canvassing of neighborhoods, and checking out other rapes, robberies and murders looking for something that might be similar what happened at Fagiani's.

They'd eventually identified the carnival mechanic reputed to have been Andrews' sometimes boyfriend. He'd lost his job due to alcohol issues and moved to the South where they lost track of him. But, as Winegar noted, the timeline of his movements didn't jibe with the evidence and he'd been crossed off the suspect list.

He also saw where Jarecki had found Liston Beal in April 1990 living in Oklahoma. He even visited the man and obtained fingerprints and hair samples. However, the fingerprints didn't match any of those found at the murder scene, nor could any of the witnesses pick him out of a photo lineup.

After putting the case file in order, making notes as he went along, Winegar began using the internet to see if he could locate the witnesses and law enforcement personnel mentioned in the files. He discovered that quite a few had passed away, including two of the men who'd been in the bar on the night of the murder.

However, Winegar was excited to learn that the third man, David Luce, was still alive and living in a healthcare facility in Chico, California. If the investigation reports were correct, Luce was the one man who might actually be able to identify the stranger sitting at the bar. But the detective's excitement was tempered; he had a possible eyewitness, but no suspect.

Winegar was also surprised to find out that the original criminalist, Peter Barnett, was not only still alive, but working for his own company, Forensic Science Associates. The detective had been impressed with Barnett's thorough processing of the crime scene. The photographs he'd taken of the bar matched Luce's story about the man with the Southern drawl sitting on a stool at the far end, smoking a cigarette. If there was ever a trial, having a living witness who could walk a jury through the crime scene and the evidence was far better than reading from reports.

Interior of Fagiani's bar showing stool pulled away from the bar. The "stranger" suspected of murdering Anita Andrews was last seen by witnesses sitting on the stool. Photo courtesy of the Napa County District Attorney's Office.

Reviewing the material, Winegar saw that in 2001, one of the last detectives to work on the case, Peter Jerich, had attended a DNA cold case class in December 2001 put on by the California Department of Justice. Jerich had talked about the case with other officers and the criminalist teaching the class, Bruce Moran, who asked Jerich to send some of the evidence—specifically the towel found on the floor beneath the sink and the hair samples taken from Liston Beal—to the DOJ crime laboratory. The evidence was sent in December 2001.

However, according to a report in the binders from Jerich, when he contacted the laboratory in October 2004, the material had not yet been tested. Current cases with suspects took precedence and the lab had simply been too busy to work on an old cold case. The detective, who soon transferred out of investigations, was told in December 2004 that the work would be done.

It was now May 2006 and Winegar couldn't locate any results of the testing in the binders. So he placed a call to the criminalist listed on the report, Michelle Terra. He was told that she was on maternity leave and the evidence had not been examined.

In July, however, he received a call from Terra. The towel had tested positive for male DNA, however, the DNA was "degraded" and would need to be sent to a private laboratory with better equipment for further examination.

Degraded DNA meant that it was missing some of the attributes that could absolutely link the hit to a suspect within the necessary legal framework of "reasonable scientific certainty." A number of factors can result in degraded DNA: the passage of time, or exposure to the elements, or contamination from other DNA sources or substances. However, while it wasn't as good as a high quality DNA hit, it could be used to exclude an individual, or in court it could be put into evidence as "similar" to a suspect's DNA.

The towel was sent to the Serological Research Institute. On April 16, 2007, Winegar received both bad news and good news.

The bad news was that the degraded sample didn't meet the standards necessary to be uploaded to the FBI's Combined DNA Index System, more commonly known as CODIS. Using the system, qualified DNA profiles from crime scenes, as well as samples taken from convicted offenders and arrestees, are stored in a computer database that can be quickly identified and matched. So the DNA from the towel wasn't going to be compared to the DNA of known criminals and other crime scenes stored in CODIS.

The good news, however, was that the sample was enough to once and for all eliminate Liston Beal as a suspect. Even though detective Jarecki had established that Beal's fingerprints weren't on any of the evidence from the bar, and none of the witnesses had picked him out of the lineup; he'd remained the only name on the suspect list.

One of the first things Winegar did after the call from Terra was get in touch with Muriel Fagiani. The detective thought eliminating Beal as a suspect was a big step in the process. One more box checked off the list of things to do. He thought Muriel would be happy to know it, too.

After he first picked up the case in 2006, he'd called Muriel to let her know he was actively working on it. Now in her 80s, Muriel was still something of a legend in Napa both as a community activist and as the woman who owned Fagiani's, which she'd kept closed even as the city grew around it. Within the department, she was the woman with the wild gray hair who wouldn't let them forget that her sister's murder had never been solved.

As much as Winegar had been assigned to the case because it was an unresolved murder that deserved his attention, there was no denying there was a little bit of wanting to get her off the department's back. So when he started, it was to be able to show her, and the public, that every single thing from scientific and investigative standpoints was being done. If nothing came of it, the department, and perhaps Muriel, could rest easy that they'd tried everything.

After his first call, Muriel contacted him every week or two for updates. She was always polite, but she was also upfront and had her own ideas on who could have done the murder, and Liston Beal was one of those. So he thought she might want to know that Beal was off the list. However, her reaction was that all that meant was they still didn't know who killed her sister.

Shaking his head, Winegar went back to work. The bar towel DNA wasn't good enough for CODIS. But he wondered what might be revealed if other items found at the scene, such as the cigarette butt and the screwdriver/murder weapon, were tested. He knew from talking to Terra that the backlog at the DOJ crime lab was extensive and filled with current cases, but with a little persistence and friendly pleading on his part, she agreed to test the items.

On November 29, 2007, he sent her blood and hair samples, the screwdriver, broken glass from the bottle used to strike Anita, and the single cigarette butt collected from the ashtray. It was almost two years before he heard back. He didn't blame Terra or the DOJ laboratory, he knew they were busy and he was too busy with a full caseload to be the squeaky wheel.

Then on September 30, 2009, Terra called to say she'd examined the evidence. The results were negative for most of the items he'd sent. But not only was there DNA evidence on the cigarette butt, but it was a good hit with the suspect's full DNA profile that would definitely hold up in court. All he needed was a suspect to compare it to, and for that, Terra said she would be uploading the data to CODIS.

The cigarette butt data joined a large pool. As of June 30, 2009, according to FBI statistics, there were more than 7 million offender DNA profiles, and 272,000 forensic DNA profiles from crime scene samples, uploaded to CODIS. The result had been more than 93,000 hits.

On November 5, 2009, Terra called Winegar again. This time her voice was excited. "We got a hit!" The DNA belonged to Roy Melanson, a convicted murderer serving time in a Colorado penitentiary. As Winegar later learned, after his conviction for Michele Wallace's murder in 1994, Melanson was returned to Kentucky to complete his prison term there.

Then in May 2003, he was sent back to Colorado to begin serving his sentence for murder. Upon his arrival at the Colorado Department of Corrections prison, his DNA was obtained and entered into the CODIS databank.

This cigarette butt left in an ashtray at Fagiani's bar on July 10, 1974 would lead to the conviction of Roy Melanson for the murder of Anita Andrews 37 years later. Photo courtesy of the Napa County District Attorney's Office.

Winegar could hardly believe what he was hearing. The dream of any homicide detective was cracking a big case, especially an old unsolved case. It was getting late in his career—he intended to retire in a few years—and while he'd put other killers away, there was nothing in his past like solving a murder that had haunted his community for 35 years.

Hanging up with Terra, Winegar let his boss know the good news, which quickly made its way up the chain of command. He was told there would be no more working the case in his spare time, he was on it 24/7.

Now the work began in earnest. It was one thing to have a real suspect, but he still had to put the case together and present it to the Napa County District Attorney's Office for prosecution.

Ironically, after 35 years there was now a sense of urgency about putting together a case against Roy Melanson. He'd been sentenced in Colorado under laws that were in effect back in 1974, which meant he was up for parole in 2012. It didn't mean that he would be let out by the parole board, but it also wouldn't be the first time Melanson had found a way to avoid punishment or serving his full sentence.

Winegar had read about Melanson's long criminal history supplied to him by the California Department of Justice. The man was obviously a serial rapist and killer, a sociopath who'd spend more of his life in prison than out. But as alarming as his record was, the way he'd simply walked away from justice in some of his cases was incomprehensible. He'd been accused of rape in 1972, but avoided punishment by simply moving to a different part of Texas. Then in 1974, the victim had testified at a preliminary hearing about how he'd raped her for days and threatened to kill her, and yet he'd been allowed to make bail and left the state.

The consequences of that had been unspeakable horrors for others. Fleeing the rape warrant in Texas, he'd moved to Arizona and after a fight with his pregnant girlfriend left her in April 1974. Three months later, he'd murdered Anita Andrews in Napa, and who knew what he'd done during the prior three months.

Then fifty days after killing Anita, he'd murdered Michele Wallace. What had he done between California and Colorado?

In 1994, shortly after he'd killed Wallace, Melanson had been brought back to Texas and convicted for the rape. But instead of serving a life sentence for a habitual offender—and not just any burglar or car thief but a vicious brutal serial rapist and suspected murderer—he'd got the habitual offender sentence overturned and served twelve years.

Then three months after getting out of prison in Texas, he was the only suspect in the disappearance of Pauline Klumpp. Again, it was doubtful he'd been a law-abiding gentleman during those three months—Winegar had not found a single instance of real employment and instead Melanson seemed to have lived his whole life living off of and preying on others. And God only knew what he'd done between Klumpp disappearing and his incarceration in Kentucky.

Another alarming trend was evident from looking at Melanson's case history. As time went on, he'd grown more dangerous. He was a serial rapist who'd learned that leaving his victims alive could mean prison. So after fleeing the rape warrant in Texas, he'd killed Anita Andrews, Michele Wallace, and in all likelihood, Pauline Klumpp.

How many other victims were there? No one but Melanson could say. But Winegar knew he needed to be stopped, permanently.

XXI

November 30, 2009

Flying to Colorado, Winegar's goal was to get a new DNA sample and fingerprints from Roy Melanson, as well as a writing sample to compare to the 1974 gas station receipt. Just to confirm what he already knew—it would match the evidence from Fagiani's bar. There was "no way in hell" he thought a serial killer like Melanson would talk to him.

Still, he, Sgt. Cantillon and Napa County Deputy District Attorney Paul Gero debated what Melanson would say if he did. There were three options: he could deny the murder; he could admit it, including that it was "self-defense" after Andrews attacked him; or he could use "common sense" to explain why his DNA and fingerprints were there by saying he'd stopped at the bar for a drink and a smoke then left.

Winegar was happy that Gero had been assigned to prosecute the case. They'd known each other since they were both early in their careers; he was working sex crimes against juveniles, and Gero was prosecuting those cases. He both liked and respected Gero.

Arriving at the Fort Lyon Correctional Facility, the three men from Napa were surprised because other than a high fence around it, the prison looked more like a college campus, including dorms and grassy areas where they could see unescorted inmates strolling casually around. They knew the facility was for inmates with long-term health issues.

But still, it wasn't exactly the sort of place they would have envisioned keeping a sociopathic serial killer who'd fled warrants as easily as some people cross the street, then raped and killed women while on the loose.

They were taken to an office where Winegar could sit down with Melanson while the conversation was being recorded. Gero and Cantillon waited in another room listening in.

When Melanson arrived, wearing a confused look because he hadn't been told what he was being summoned for, Winegar shook his hand and invited him to have a seat next to the door. He then sat across from him and took a moment to size the man up.

Winegar was a little surprised by Melanson's appearance. He'd seen photographs of Melanson as a much younger, thinner man, not the big, bear-like, 72-year-old with the bald head and round grizzled face.

Introducing himself, he said, "I'm a detective with the Napa Police Department."

"Where is that, Napa?" Melanson asked innocently.

"It's in California."

"Okay."

"And I wanted to talk to you about an investigation I'm conducting out there. But before I do, I need to let you know that like you're not in my custody here or anything like that," Winegar said. "And there's the door. Anytime you don't want to talk to me, you're free to go. Okay?"

Although he said it matter-of-factly, Winegar had discussed this important beginning with Gero before arriving. The detective didn't think Melanson would talk to him at all, but he was certain the crafty old inmate would shut down immediately if he read him his Miranda warnings that he had the right to remain silent and have an attorney present. But Miranda warnings only have to be given to a suspect if he's in custody, or believes that he's in custody for the crime he's being questioned about.

By making sure that Melanson understood he wasn't in custody and was free to leave, Gero was certain that he didn't have to read him his rights. And it would allow whatever Melanson might say into evidence during a trial.

"I got nothing to hide," Melanson said.

Winegar, who didn't want to jump right in with accusations of murder, started with a soft question, asking if Melanson had ever been to California. The old man shrugged and said he'd been to Needles once when he was living in Tucson.

"Have you ever heard of Napa?" Winegar asked.

"Yeah, I've heard of Napa Valley on television," Melanson replied.

"So you've never been there?"

"Not to my knowledge," Melanson said. "Not in this life."

"Not in this life?" Winegar repeated. "Well, then, really, it's gonna be a short interview. I was gonna talk to you about the time you were in Napa Valley, in Napa, in the city of Napa."

"I have never been there," Melanson repeated.

Winegar changed the subject. "They don't walk you around when you're in this prison?"

"Oh, no," Melanson said. "I can roam freely."

"You just roam freely and everything?" Winegar repeated the statement for the recording to once again emphasize that there was nothing, and nobody like a guard, keeping Melanson from leaving if he wanted. "Oh, that is so cool, because when we saw you walking over, I went, 'Hmm,' because in California, you know, I think they have guards and stuff like that and everything."

"Well, I'm not a threat," Melanson said, then repeated himself. "I'm not a threat."

After a series of other questions about Melanson's age and background, Winegar got back to business. "I'm talking about a crime that happened in 1974 in Napa. Okay?"

"What is that? Thirty-five years ago?" Melanson said. "All of '74 I was here in the mountains. I was working for Frank Spadafora."

As Melanson continued his denials and explanations, Winegar didn't mention the DNA or fingerprint evidence. Instead, he told Melanson that he'd come up with his name in the course of his investigation and due to a television crime drama about the Michele Wallace case.

"So what I'm investigating was a murder, is a murder that happened in Napa at Fagiani's Bar, 813 Main Street, in July of '74, sometime between the 10th and the 11th of 1974. Okay? And as a matter of fact, they even made one of those crime dramas off your case? Have you ever seen it?"

"Yes, sir."

"So your name came up to me, and so I'm here investigating it to see if possibly you had anything to do with that homicide, the killing of—what happened is she was pretty brutally stabbed with an object, and I wanted to see if you had anything to do with that," Winegar said.

Melanson shook his head. "I swear to God, I never did. I hate to hear something like that, and I'm very, very serious about that. I was raised different. I know what I'm here for now but I was raised different than that. I swear to God and I'm not an atheist. I believe in God."

Winegar asked Melanson if he smoked. The old man said he had in his youth but stopped as a teenager. He then swore up and down again that he'd been in the mountains working for Spadafora all of the summer of 1974.

As they were talking, Winegar's cell phone went off several times. It was Gero and Cantillon texting him with questions they wanted to ask, but he explained to Melanson that it was his son and wife texting. Apparently, Melanson, who'd spent the past twenty years in prison, had never seen a cell phone up close and was intrigued by its small size and the ability to type messages on it.

After a few minutes, Winegar interrupted the flow of the conversation to note that the science of crime-fighting had come a long way since 1974, especially fingerprinting and DNA comparison. "You ever hear of DNA?"

"Yes, sir. I watch television."

"If you sweat, they can get it. If you spit on something. A piece of paper, a glass you had, you know, and if you were having a drink in a bar that would have your DNA on it, you know?"

The subject seemed to disturb Melanson who took the conversation in another direction, which Winegar allowed for a few minutes before bringing it back.

"Well, the crime I'm investigating is a cold case. Do you know what a cold case homicide is?"

Melanson nodded. He knew what it was because he'd been the subject on one on a television show and that was why Winegar was talking to him. "Somebody probably saw my picture on that and said, 'Whoa. Look at here, and look at the record on that bird.' I'm so tired of that. I'm thinking very seriously about some lawsuits. They're saying the wrong thing. They're lying on there."

"What about what I'm investigating?" Winegar interrupted. "This would have been in July, fifty days before the one that supposedly happened in Gunnison ... in Napa, California ... a female bartender was killed brutally. Okay?"

When Melanson hemmed and hawed through general statements about DNA testing and fingerprint evidence,

Winegar decided it was time to confront him. "What would you say if we had your DNA in that crime scene in Napa at 813 Main Street?

The charm dropped out of Melanson's Texas drawl. "I'd say it's wrong," he said tensely. "I'd say it cannot be."

"Cannot be?" Winegar asked.

Melanson nodded. "Definitely cannot be."

"Well, you know what DNA is. It's pretty open and shut."

Ever the jailhouse lawyer, Melanson countered. "Well, not necessarily, because I just got through reading a paper, where they had found this one woman—I think it was in the eastern states over there—where she had falsified hundreds of cases of DNA."

Melanson was obviously concerned enough about DNA evidence to read up on it. "What about fingerprints?" he asked.

"I think the DNA is probably more sophisticated than the fingerprints."

"I mean, what if we found your fingerprints there?"

"You didn't find my fingerprints there."

Winegar tried to bait Melanson with other options for killing Andrews, such as self-defense. "So if somebody came at you and you were trying to mess with them, pick them up or whatever, and they thought something wrong and they were attacking you, then self-defense—that would be a defense. Do you understand what I'm saying?"

But Melanson wasn't buying it. "I couldn't have been in that bar."

"So you're just saying you were not in that bar?"

"Well, I was here," Melanson said. "How could I be two different places? And I don't even know where Napa Valley is."

"So if we have blood evidence and we have DNA ..."

"You ain't got mine."

Winegar changed the subject to Melanson's time in the Texas prison, but the inmate was starting to get testy.

"That's all behind me there," he scowled. "My God. I'm trying my best to forget all that shit. I'm 72 years old. My God. Can't I … can't I have a few years of …"

This time it was Winegar who cut him off. "How's your health?"

"It's not good at all. I got heart problems. I got diabetes, this COPD."

After a series of other off-the-topic questions and answers, Melanson started talking about working for Spadafora and that he felt bad about shooting a mother bear with cubs. "I shot one time, and it went to screaming and hollering and coming back toward me. But I would have went and pulled out bullets. I swear to God in heaven I would have pulled the bullets out and made her well if I'd had that power, because I was hurt—you know, it was hurting, and I would have made her well like that, because she was brown and coming back. She was gonna come put a stop to that hurt, where it was coming, yes, sir."

Winegar didn't know what the bear story was supposed to reveal about Melanson. Maybe that he was a compassionate soul, and therefore couldn't be a cold-blooded serial killer. The detective wasn't buying it.

When the subject came back around to the murder in Napa, Melanson was again adamant that he wasn't involved. "On my dead mother's grave, I had nothing to do with anything that you have discussed. And I mean that. I'm getting so old, I'll die anytime now. You know, I've lived a full life, not a good life, but from what you say, I'm not capable of that. And nor was I capable of it even back then. … Mom and Daddy raised me different. On a lot of things I just didn't do right, but they raised me right."

Melanson again brought up the topic of lawsuits and said he was going to file a civil rights suit because there'd been no cause of death established in the Michele Wallace case. Then he asked if there was a cause of death established for the case in Napa. "There's a cause of death, and your DNA is all over that cause of death. Your DNA is there."

Melanson shook his head. "It ain't mine," he said. "I don't care what you got. It wasn't me. I wasn't there. And I don't guess there's anything in this world that's foolproof."

"Well, DNA is pretty foolproof," Winegar countered. He said he was giving Melanson one more chance to explain why the evidence pointed to him.

Melanson asked if he was "wanted" in Napa for the murder. But Winegar didn't answer. He just hit him with a series of questions. Did he take things from the bar? Did he take the car? All of which the inmate denied.

The detective took off the gloves. "Here's what I want you to know. I didn't just pick you out from random. I had never heard of you in my life. I'm a cold case investigator, homicide investigator. Your DNA came up as being there. Okay? I didn't just pick you at random. That's not the way the system works. I came here to talk to Roy Melanson. And all the sciences, all the everything, points at you, and so I need you to explain it in a better way than, 'It wasn't me.'"

Melanson, who throughout the questioning had maintained a polite, good ol' boy demeanor, was finally pushed to the edge. "Then I'll explain it with an attorney. If I'm gonna be accused of something like that when I wasn't even there and can prove I wasn't there, then I'm gonna get an attorney, because I am tired of this."

The interview was officially over.

XXII

April 2010

Roy Melanson might have been trying to forget "all that shit" he'd done, but never taken any responsibility for, and wishing to be left alone for a few years. But his past wasn't going to let him.

Even as Don Winegar and Paul Gero, with the help of Napa County DA investigator Leslie Severe, were putting together their case, the CODIS databank came up with another hit on Melanson. In the spring 2010, the state police in Louisiana were entering DNA data from old cold cases when CODIS notified them there was a suspect match to a case from 1988 in Livingston Parish.

The DNA samples had been taken from the body of Charlotte Sauerwin. They'd been matched to the DNA samples that Melanson had been forced to give when he entered the Colorado prison system.

Notified of the suspect profile match, Stanley Carpenter, who'd been the chief of detectives for the Livingston Parish Sheriff's Office since 2007, recalled the case immediately. He'd been a narcotics detective when the murder occurred but it was a big case in a small jurisdiction like Livingston Parish.

One of Carpenter's first tasks after receiving the DNA report was to contact the people who knew and loved Charlotte the best. Her parents had died not knowing who killed their daughter, even though they'd suspected her fiancé. But he was able to reach out to the victim's sister, Charlene, and Vince LeJeune.

Life had been hard on LeJeune. He'd dealt with Charlotte's death by not dealing with it. First with hard drugs until after his daughter was born in 1990. While he'd never gone back to that lifestyle, he did get a prescription for the anti-depressant Xanax and ate it like candy.

Even though he remained gainfully employed, the next twenty-two years saw him go through a series of failed marriages and relationships. He didn't blame the women; he knew he was hard to live with. But how much of that had to do with Charlotte's death and the cloud of suspicion that had followed him ever since, he didn't know. He was only 24 years old when she was murdered and he was suspected. There'd never been a chance to find out what life would have been like—what he would have been like--otherwise.

Part of that was due to the old chief of detectives, Kernie Foster. The man had never outright accused him of being the killer to his face. But Vince had heard from other people that Foster flat out told them: "That boy killed that girl and I'm gonna catch him."

In some ways, it didn't matter that Foster never was able to bring charges against him. An entire town full of people, some of them friends, had judged him guilty and turned their backs on him. There might not have been any walls or bars holding him in, but he was in a prison of sorts.

As time passed, it got a little easier to be anonymous in Walker. The town's population doubled. It got a Wal-Mart, a Winn Dixie, a McDonalds, and four strip malls. But for long-time residents, and people who met them, he was the mad dog who brutally killed his fiancé.

At times it had made him angry. One girlfriend told him that a man in town warned her to get away from him because he was a killer. "I'm not," he told her, "but you tell him that if I hear of that coming out of his mouth again, I will be."

Coupled with the anger was a deep sense of guilt. After Charlotte died, he used to visit her grave three or four times a year to talk to her. He felt like he'd failed her. He'd promised to keep her safe, but she'd been murdered. That was sometimes tougher to live with than the whispers and accusations in people's eyes.

There were times when he probably owed his life to the same handful of friends, and his family, who had stuck with him from the beginning. That family included his two daughters; the one born in 1990, after he gained custody of her four years later; and another born eight years later.

There was a game he used to play when he was alone with a .357 magnum revolver. He'd put one bullet in the cylinder and spin it, then cock the hammer back and look to see where the bullet ended up. But he had people who loved him and counted on him, so as often as that bullet might have come up in that .357, he never pulled the trigger.

Vince LeJeune lived for 22 years under the cloud of suspicion, falsely believed to have murdered his fiancé. Photo courtesy of Vince LeJeune.

Vince tried to be the best father he could and that included being completely honest with his girls. He might have been stricter than some fathers; then again, he knew more about the evil in the world than most. But they always knew that if he was a little hard on them, and their boyfriends, it was because he loved them and wanted to keep them safe.

He never hid anything from his daughters. Not the drugs. Not the drinking. Not what had happened to Charlotte. When they got old enough to ask about her, he showed them pictures of the two of them and told them. He figured they'd hear about it at school or on the streets eventually; though if they were ever given a hard time about it, they never told him.

LeJeune had given up on the police ever catching Charlotte's killer. But that all changed one evening in April 2010. He was at his best friend's house drinking a few beers with his buddies when his dad called. Someone named Stan Carpenter with the sheriff's department was looking for him.

"He say what for?" he asked suspiciously. Even though Kernie Foster had retired, he wouldn't have been surprised if someone wanted to ask him more questions.

"All he'd tell me was it has something to do with Charlotte's death."

"Here we go again," LeJeune told his friends as he hung up and then called Carpenter.

"This is Vince LeJeune," he said when the detective answered. "I hear you're looking for me."

"I'd like you to come down to the sheriff's office tomorrow, there's been a break in the Charlotte Sauerwin case," Carpenter said.

LeJeune rolled his eyes at his friends. There'd been other false alarms and he thought it could even be a trick to get him to the police station so they could interrogate him some more. But then the detective told him that a prisoner in Colorado was a match for DNA found on Charlotte.

It wasn't what he was expecting to hear. He started crying and then to his buddies' alarm fell completely apart.

After he pulled himself together, they all talked about it for awhile. Then he just wanted to go home and be alone. As he drove back to his place, he got to thinking about the times the police lied to him or tried to trick him into saying something. He wondered if the meeting with Carpenter the next day would be more of the same.

However, when he arrived he was ushered into Carpenter's office and was surprised to see Charlene there. Her family had treated him like a pariah since the murder and the tension between the two of them as they sat several chairs apart from each other was palpable.

Then Carpenter told them what had transpired with the DNA test. After all those years, it turned out that a serial rapist and murderer now serving time in Colorado was the man Charlotte met at the Laundromat. He'd preyed on her hopes of getting the land cleared so that she and Vince could build their dream house. Then he'd raped, beat and strangled her before slitting her throat.

It also turned out that he'd been caught with Charlotte's little .380 Beretta. Apparently he'd tried to file the serial number off but the police had been able to recover all but one of them. Unfortunately, that had not been enough to trace the gun back to Louisiana though it would now matter if his case went to trial.

Sitting in his chair, Vince couldn't believe it. The long wait was over. He got up and hugged Charlene and they cried together. He wasn't ready to forgive her or her family or the town that had judged him guilty without a trial, but at that moment it felt good to share the tears.

On April 10, Stan Carpenter and detective Ben Bourgeois of Livingston Parish flew to Colorado. Like the team from Napa, they wanted to get fresh DNA samples from Melanson and see if he would talk to them.

At first Melanson joked with them about being a Cajun, like Bourgeois, not knowing that would tie into what another witness had told the investigators back in 1988. But when they brought up the subject of DNA and Charlotte Sauerwin, he said he was through talking.

Melanson smiled at them and said that if they could find his DNA on their victim, "you go ahead and charge me."

The detectives smiled back. "We will."

XXIII

The two men sat in their wheelchairs facing each other across the Napa County courtroom. One, Roy Melanson, obese and wearing thick, black-framed glasses on his round, bald head, dressed in a button-down shirt, a tie and slacks, showed little emotion next to the defense table. The other, David Luce, dying of cancer at age 67, oxygen tubes in his nose and attached to a portable tank, was happy to be on the witness stand doing this one last good thing before he passed.

It was the second day of the trial for the 74-year-old Melanson, who'd been charged with first-degree murder. And it had been thirty-seven years since they'd last looked upon each other's face.

In his opening statements on the first day, Gero told the eight men and four women on the jury that the case was about "a brutal murder and the progress of forensic science." Police investigators had initially done all they could to solve the crime, he said, but the case had gone cold for thirty years until DNA from the crime scene led to Roy Melanson.

Gero touched on Winegar's interview with Melanson and how the convicted killer said he'd never been in Napa, or Fagiani's, or met Andrews. "He denied everything," Gero said. "He even swore on his mother's grave."

The prosecutor told the jurors they would be hearing about other crimes Melanson had committed, including rape and murder. "I'll ask you to find the defendant, Roy Melanson, guilty of the murder of Anita Andrews," he'd concluded.

However, Melanson's public defender, Allison Wilensky, assured the jurors it was a "reasonable doubt case." The DNA evidence, she said, was very weak. And there was "no way of knowing" who the last man to leave the bar was that night.

"I'll ask you to return a verdict of 'not guilty,'" she said.

Gero had then begun the People's case by calling Joe Moore, the first police officer on the scene, who recalled meeting a "shocked but calm," Muriel Fagiani who showed him the body in the storeroom.

In an attempt to demonstrate to the jurors all the work that had gone into the case, Gero had then called detectives Bailey and Jarecki to the stand to describe their efforts, leading up to detective Jerich and the work he'd done until 2004.

Criminalist Peter Barnett was called to the stand to detail how he found the crime scene on the morning after the murder. Using photographs taken on that morning, he described how the blood-splatter on the walls and throughout the storeroom demonstrated the violence of the crime as Anita Andrews was beat and stabbed with the screwdriver.

Referring to other photographs, he noted how the placement of the stool and the ashtray on the otherwise clean bar, indicated that Andrews had not yet had a chance to finish up where the stranger had been sitting. But she had one of her high heels on when her body was found in the storeroom, which indicated that she wanted to leave.

Watching the proceedings from the first row behind the prosecution table, Don Winegar recalled how happy he'd been when he found out that Joe Moore and Barnett were still alive and able to testify. Besides showing the chain of custody, there was the human aspect.

Then as Luce was wheeled by a bailiff up next to the witness stand, Winegar remembered the day in January 2010 he met the man. It was a little over a month after returning from Colorado and his interview with Melanson, and he'd called Luce first and told him what was going on and asked if they could meet.

The "peacemaker" at Fagiani's on the night of July 10, 1974 was excited to hear that at long last the case was solved. He said he'd be happy to help in any way possible, but the detective better hurry; he had terminal cancer and was living in a long-term healthcare facility in Chico, California.

On January 6, 2010, Winegar drove the two hours to Chico where Luce met him at the door of his apartment in the healthcare facility. He was smoking a cigarette while hooked up to a portable oxygen tank. But he smiled and invited Winegar in like a long, lost friend, and they spent the first fifteen minutes talking about Napa in the 70s and their lives.

Winegar liked the gregarious Luce. He was a tough guy and had lived a tough life, but he laughed easily and clearly enjoyed talking about old times. Then they turned to the night of July 10, 1974.

Luce said he was married when he moved to Napa in 1969 and worked construction with the two friends, both of whom had since died, he was carousing with that night. They'd already been to several other bars, including The Happy Hour bar where he left his truck. Then they stopped by Fagiani's for a beer on the way to another bar. He remembered the stranger at the end of the bar schmoozing Anita, and how his friend hadn't like the way the guy sat with his back to them and tried to hide his face.

The friend had yelled at the man. But as they were getting ready to leave, Luce had played the peacemaker and gone up to the stranger and told him they meant no harm as he shook the man's hand.

Luce described the man's face to Winegar as *"demure,"* by which the detective assumed meant that he wasn't aggressive-looking. He also said the stranger's hands were "soft, hot and wimpy."

"The only other person I ever met who shook hands like that was Richard Nixon," he said with a laugh, adding that he'd met the former president at a rally.

As Luce reminisced, Winegar was struck by how exactly his story matched the photograph of the bar. The barstools lined up neatly under the counter, except for the stool on the end. The counter itself wiped clean but for an ashtray, a shot glass and a spoon. That sort of corroboration would be important at a trial.

After Luce told his story, Winegar asked if he'd be willing to view a photo lineup he'd brought with him. A great deal of effort had gone into creating the lineup so that all six of the photos were similar—black and white, cropped the same just below the chin, and nothing in the background to giveaway location. He told the old man that the suspect may or may not be in the photograph and to only identify someone if he was sure.

With that admonition, Winegar laid out the sheet with the photographs on it in front of Luce, who carefully scanned each for several seconds though it seemed much longer to Winegar.

Then Luce pointed to one. *"That's him."*

Winegar did his best to hide his excitement. Luce had just identified Roy Melanson as the stranger at the end of the bar. "How do you know?" he asked calmly.

"The eyes," Luce replied. *"I remember the eyes."*

Gero had indicted Melanson for first degree murder in April 2010. The original trial date had been set for April 2011, but when it was pushed back to September, Gero had worried that Luce might not make it. So they'd taken the extraordinary step of videotaping his testimony in an empty courtroom as Gero and Melanson's public defender Wilensky asked questions. That way they'd be able to use his statement in court if he died.

However, Luce was alive and his voice was strong as he recounted the night he first saw Melanson, who he described as then being in his 40s with a receding hairline and thin lips. He sat on the barstool, "crossing his legs like a girl."

It was clear to Luce and his friends that Melanson was purposefully shielding his face with his hand as he sat smoking and drinking. His friend had become angry and started shouting insults at the stranger. "How come you're hiding your face?" Luce yelled in the courtroom, imitating his friend.

On the way out of the bar, Luce said, he went over to shake the man's hand. Winegar smiled as he repeated his story about President Nixon and the jurors laughed.

After Luce stepped down, Winegar was called to the stand to discuss all of his efforts leading up to the DNA testing. He told the jurors that the toughest part of the investigation had been trying to track down 150 witnesses, many of them having died.

Some of those witnesses were in Texas and Louisiana where Winegar, Gero and Napa County DAO investigator Leslie Severe had gone because the prosecutor was going to try to get evidence of "prior bad acts" into the trial. Normally, evidence of a defendant's previous crimes wouldn't be admissible at trial. However, in certain instances, particularly dealing with sexual serial killers where the prosecution could show a "common plan or scheme," higher courts had ruled that such testimony could be used to show the defendant committed his crimes in a similar fashion, including choosing similar victims. In this case, they were showing that he was a robber, a rapist, as well as a murderer.

The Napa County team had interviewed the woman Melanson had raped in 1974. His victim from 1972 had died, and Melanson had fled before he was tried in the case. However, they obtained transcripts of her testimony from the preliminary hearing, hoping to be able to use it. They'd also obtained reports of the rape he'd committed in 1962.

They'd also talked to detectives in Colorado about the Michele Wallace case and obtained the testimony of Chuck Matthews, who had since died, from the trial.

Pursuing all of Melanson's criminal history, they'd also traveled to Louisiana. About the same time Melanson was indicted in California, they'd heard about the CODIS hit linking him to the murder of Charlotte Sauerwin in Livingston, Parish. So they'd talked to chief of detectives Stanley Carpenter about that case.

While there, they'd also had a chance to meet Vince LeJeune, the fiancé of the victim who for many years had been the chief suspect. He told Severe that his life had been "ruined." And Winegar couldn't believe how he'd been treated.

After testifying about his efforts leading up to the DNA, Winegar was asked to step down, subject to recall for his testimony later about his interview with Melanson. Gero had then called Michele Terra to the stand to testify about the DNA tests.

After the initial hit, Terra had been asked to test the rest of the evidence—nearly fifty items—to see if there would be anymore connections. It wasn't just to see if there would be more links to Melanson; the prosecution also had to make sure the defense attorney couldn't accuse them of not having tested evidence that could have pointed to another suspect. But there were not more matches.

During her cross examination of Terra, Wilensky had challenged the DNA results from the towel as weak and also contaminated. Both of which Terra conceded, though on redirect by Gero, she contended that it wouldn't change her findings, especially not the absolutely certain hit from the cigarette butt.

Napa Police Detective Don Winegar, Napa District Attorney's investigator Leslie Severe, and Napa County Deputy District Attorney Paul Gero made sure Melanson was convicted for the murder of Anita Andrews. Photo courtesy of the Napa County District Attorney's Office.

On the third day of trial, the jurors walked across the street to Fagiani's to view the scene of the crime. They were accompanied by Judge Guadangni in his black robe, the attorneys, three bailiffs, and a court reporter, as well as Winegar and Severe. Melanson had declined to be rolled across the street in his wheelchair.

The bar had finally been sold to a developer who was renovating the interior with plans to reopen as Fagiani's. Extensive remodeling was already underway when the jurors walked through the doors, but Gero had brought the black and white photographs of the interior as it appeared on the morning Andrews' body was found.

Going into the bar it was as if stepping back into time. Winegar was thankful that Muriel Fagiani had kept the bar basically in the same condition. And here the jury was able to view the crime scene, just as she'd planned.

After his interview with Melanson, the one person he'd most looked forward to talking to was Muriel Fagiani. It was going to be *his moment*, when the hard-working detective got to tell the victim's sister that he'd solved the case.

Not letting on that he had big news, he'd called Muriel and asked her to come to the office for an update. When she arrived, he sat her down in a chair and solemnly announced, "We have a suspect." He told her about Roy Melanson and the evidence against him and waited for what he thought would be an emotional outpouring of gratitude and relief.

Instead, she'd looked at him with a blank face and said, *"It won't bring her back."* But she did want to know if she could go talk to Melanson and ask him why he murdered her sister.

At first, Winegar was stunned by her reaction. Then he got it. For him, the case had been a challenge, a cold case detectives' dream; sure he got deep satisfaction knowing that a killer who had committed a heinous crime so many years ago was going to face justice, but that was his job.

Sitting in front of him, however, was an old woman who had lived with the emotional toll of her sister's murder for 35 years. She'd walked into the storeroom and saw the blood and the body. She'd lived with the thought that the killer might still be in Napa, even a neighbor or someone she passed on the street. Instead of spending Christmases and birthdays with her sister, she'd spent the last three decades trying not to let her murder be forgotten.

It was his job to find out *who* did it. It was more important to her to know *why*.

Unfortunately, she would never know. Not that anyone expected Melanson to take the stand and explain his actions, but Muriel had died December 9, 2010,

As the jurors walked through the bar where Muriel had spent much of her childhood, the last place she'd seen her sister alive, Winegar wondered how Melanson ever got to that little bar from Orange, Texas.

After the tour, Judge Guadangni adjourned court for the weekend. They picked up again on Monday with the jury watching and listening to the 40-minute interview between Winegar and Melanson at the Fort Lyon Correctional Facility. They were also given a transcript to make it easier to follow.

There was one last thing he'd asked of Melanson before they parted that day. He asked him to sign his name on a piece of paper. The reason became clear in court when Gero introduced a copy of the gas credit card receipt from Sacramento in 1974. It wasn't a very good copy, the original had been lost, and a Napa Police Department handwriting expert could not conclude with certainty that it matched the signature Melanson had given Winegar. But it was "similar" and appeared that the man who signed the receipt was trying to disguise his writing.

The handwriting analysis was not a smoking gun, perhaps, but another piece of the puzzle. Especially when added to the DNA evidence, as well as the testimony of Janet Lipsey, a criminalist with the Napa Police Department. Following Winegar to the stand, she told the jurors that more than a dozen fingerprints had been found on bottles at the bar that matched Melanson's.

On Tuesday, Gero began calling the witnesses who were the victims of "all that shit" from his past that Melanson told Winegar he was trying to forget. Prior to the trial, the prosecutor had asked Judge Guadangni to allow seven examples of prior bad acts into evidence, including the murder of Charlotte Sauerwin, and the disappearance of Pauline Klumpp.

Defense attorney Wilensky had, of course, fought the admission of any of the priors. But Guadangni decided to allow testimony for four: the rapes Melanson committed in Texas, as well as evidence from the murder of Michele Wallace.

The victim from the 1962 rape had not been called to testify on the stand. However, Gero was allowed to have Severe read information into the record, noting that Melanson had been convicted and sentenced for the crime.

Much more dramatic, the victim of the rape in 1974, now in her 50s, appeared on the witness stand to describe the ordeal she'd gone through when just 17 years old. She looked at Melanson the entire time as she testified.

Then in graphic detail, she told the jurors about how she'd been raped in Texas and Louisiana for several days before she'd talked "the old cowboy" into letting her go. Throughout her torment, she said, the defendant had threatened to kill her. "I thought I was going to die."

Gero had then gone into the Michele Wallace case by having Napa County deputy district attorney Scott Young read Chuck Matthews' testimony from the trial. Then former undersheriff Steve Fry and Pueblo detective Jimmy Smalley testified from the stand.

Throughout the testimony of his past victims, as well as the police detectives, Melanson sat without showing any emotion. He occasionally leaned over to speak to his attorney, but that was the extent of his reaction.

Nor did he show any emotion the next day when Gero wrapped up the People's case by having Leslie Severe read the preliminary testimony given by the 1972 victim who Melanson raped and brutalized after offering to help her with a flat tire. The woman had since died never having fully recovered from the trauma.

Gero pointed out that Melanson had not been convicted in that case because he'd jumped bail and hid until his arrest for raping the other woman in 1974. Leaving the jury with that thought in mind, he rested the People's case.

Wilensky only called one witness for the defense. Its own DNA expert, Norah Rudin, who testified that the male DNA found on the bloody towel were "weak" and "very weak." The idea was to challenge the prosecution contention that Melanson used the towel to wipe his hands after washing the screwdriver off in the sink.

After that Wilensky rested her case as well. It was time for closing arguments.

Using a PowerPoint presentation, Gero reviewed the evidence: the testimony of the twenty witnesses, as well as Melanson's own statements, and the physical evidence including the DNA, fingerprints and handwriting analysis.

He urged the jurors to use their common sense as they considered the evidence. Melanson "planned" to rape Andrews, he said, which was why he shielded his face and turned his back on Luce and his friends.

Gero grew animated as he described how Andrews fought for her life. Imitating a stabbing motion, he demonstrated over and over how Melanson used the screwdriver to kill her. "This was a violent, violent way to go," he said.

Then when questioned by Winegar, the defendant had repeatedly denied even knowing where Napa was, much less having been to the bar. "He swore on his mother's grave," said Gero who replayed parts of the interview to make his points.

"He lied because he's guilty," Gero concluded before asking the jurors to find Melanson guilty of first degree murder.

Defense attorney Wilensky countered by conceding that Melanson was in the bar that night. But he was just a drifter who didn't remember all of the places he stopped on his travels. She pointed out that in 1974 Napa was not the busy tourist destination that it had become. It was just another spot on the road to her client.

Wilensky attacked the DNA evidence as weak, and the handwriting analysis as inconclusive. She didn't address Melanson's prior history for rape. But she did repeat his mantra that no cause of death had ever been established for Michele Wallace.

Apparently forgetting that she'd already conceded that Melanson was in the bar, she questioned how Luce could recall meeting him after 36 years. "You don't know what happened," she told the jurors. Some "creep" might have entered the bar after Melanson left and killed Andrews.

When Wilensky finished, Gero stood up for his rebuttal remarks. He derided Wilensky's theory as "Some Other Dude Did It." He said it was possible, "but not reasonable."

Sarcasm dripping with every word, Gero called Melanson "the truth-teller" who despite all the evidence of his prior crimes would "never do something like that" and had never been to Napa or smoked a cigarette as an adult.

And how did Melanson leave town if it wasn't in Andrews' Cadillac? He then ended his statement asking the jurors one more time for a guilty verdict.

Late on Friday afternoon, after two days of deliberations, the jury notified Guadangni that they had reached a verdict. With everyone assembled in the courtroom, waiting for the judge to read the verdict, Winegar felt his heart racing. It was all coming down to this moment. Not just all the work he'd put into the case, but 37 years of other detectives chasing leads down rabbit holes, the efforts of criminalists like Barnett and Terra.

There was also Muriel and Anita's daughter, Donna, who had lived in such fear that the killer roamed the streets of Napa that she'd moved to Hawaii and tried to live an anonymous life. And there was the community of Napa that had watched their town grow around a constant reminder that violent crime could strike anyone without notice or reason.

He was anxious. Juries could be fickle or just not see things the way a police officer or prosecutor did. They might look at Melanson and see an old man sitting in a wheelchair, not a remorseless, cold-blooded killer. However, he didn't need to worry, the jury found Roy Melanson guilty of murder.

As he had throughout the trial, Roy Melanson showed no reaction to the guilty verdict. It was as if he expected it or hardly had anything to do with him; after all, he'd spent most of his "full, not good" life in prison.

Then on October 27, any hope Melanson had of ever leaving prison if the parole board in Colorado let him go when he was eligible the next year, vanished. Guadangni sentenced him to life without the possibility of parole. He was going to be sent back to Colorado, but should that state ever release him, he'd be returned to the California Department of Corrections to serve his sentence.[12]

---

12   In 2012, Paul Gero, 40, chief deputy district attorney in the Napa County district attorney's office, was named "Outstanding Prosecutor of the Year" by the California District Attorneys Association at its annual gathering. The award noted his successful prosecution of Melanson.

EPILOGUE

As of the writing of this book, Roy Melanson is incarcerated at the Sterling Correctional Facility in Colorado. He continues to maintain his innocence for "all that shit" he's been trying to forget, either describing it as "misunderstandings," violations of his civil rights, law enforcement "prejudice" against him, and in the case of Michele Wallace, an illegal conviction based on his contention there was no established cause of death.

A jailhouse lawyer with a lot of time on his hands, Melanson has filed numerous appeals both himself and through various attorneys at one time or another. All his contentions, including about the Wallace conviction which was heard by the Colorado Supreme Court, have been rejected. That includes an appeal of his conviction for the Andrews case in which his attorney contended that the judgment must be reversed because (1) evidence of several uncharged offenses was erroneously admitted at trial; (2) this case should have been dismissed for pre-charging delay; and (3) a photographic line-up was impermissibly suggestive.

The California Court of Appeals responded in April 2013: "We reject these contentions and affirm the judgment."

Attempts to interview Melanson first for the author's 2002 book NO STONE UNTURNED, which described history and work of NecroSearch International including on the Wallace case, as well as for this book were ignored.

Another attempt to ask him questions through Matthew Watts, a producer with the Epic Mysteries television program on Investigation Discovery with whom the author was collaborating, was initially agreed to by Melanson. However, he said he would only discuss the Wallace case and no others, which was not acceptable to the author. In any event, even that interview was eventually nixed by the prison administration.

While he fights justice, the fact of the matter is that the "full, not good life" of Roy Melanson destroyed and damaged so many others. The easy victims to identify are those he raped and murdered that we know about, as well as their family members and friends. But not a single person working in law enforcement interviewed for this book believes that Melanson has been identified and held responsible for all of his violent crimes.

Detectives like Don Winegar, who left the Napa County Police Department in 2012 and now works part-time for the Napa County DAO, wonder about all those gaps in the timelines they meticulously put together for their cases. The horrible honest truth is that whenever Roy Melanson was free, he attacked women, and to believe that just because not all of his crimes were reported or linked to him is to ignore his pattern of behavior.

Potential cases against Melanson come up from time to time like putrid gas rising to the surface of swamp water. In October 2012, two investigators from Grand Junction, Colorado interviewed him in prison about a young woman from Salt Lake City whose body was found in their jurisdiction in 1974. Salt Lake City lies between California and Colorado. Melanson admitted to the investigators that he passed through Salt Lake City at that time but that was as far as they got.

In the meantime, in Livingston Parish, Louisiana, there is an active warrant for Melanson's arrest for the murder of Charlotte Sauerwin, and a detainer should he ever be released from custody in Colorado and California. However, because of his age, the other sentences, and the costs of extradition, trials and appeals, he won't be tried in Louisiana barring his release.

Still, the only way Melanson should be leaving prison is when his cold, evil heart stops beating.

"There's a special place in hell for him," Detective Stanley Carpenter of the Livingston Parish SO said.

It brings little consolation to Vince LeJeune. He refuses to feel sorry for himself despite living most of his life under that cloud of suspicion. However, he notes that no one who turned their back on him has ever offered an apology, including Kernie Foster. "Never even a 'hey, I was just doing my job,' which I could understand," he said.

When the investigators from Napa County talked to him, Leslie Severe told him he was lucky he wasn't in prison, wrongfully convicted, from the boxes of evidence she'd seen. He asked to see those boxes himself. It was clear the police had followed him for years, interviewing anyone he came into contact with. "There were maybe 15 to 30 pages dealing with other leads and information," he said. "All the rest of it, boxes and boxes, was about me."

When LeJeune was first interviewed after the DNA hits identified Melanson, his heart was full of revenge. He wanted a few minutes alone with Melanson. But now he's moving on, as he always has, keeping his true friends and family close. "I've never asked for sympathy for me," he said. "Life turned out the way it was supposed to."

In Illinois, Donna does the same with her memories of her friend, "Mush." The photographs Michele took of her still hang on the walls, and the box of letters is safe.

In the meantime, she tries not to think about Melanson though she participated in the Epic Mysteries episode. After reading the newspaper article from before the memorial service again, she wrote, "I don't even know if monster is befitting what he is. He's a soulless sub-human, who doesn't deserve to still be breathing air. Just goes to show you what a sociopath he is that he can even open his stupid mouth and say 'I'm not a monster.'"

In September 2012, Kathy Young, who now works as an investigator for a District Attorney's office west of Denver, attended the Colorado Parole Board hearing in September 2012 when they met to consider Melanson's request for parole. Prior to George Wallace Sr.'s murder, Young had promised him that she would speak for the family if Melanson ever came up for parole. She attended the hearing, a video conference with the board in Denver and Melanson in prison and addressed the board before he spoke, as well as wrote a letter opposing his release. But she chose to remain off-camera and he had no idea she was present.

"I know of at least one other agency which is currently looking at Melanson as a potential suspect in yet another murder of a young woman," Young wrote to the parole board. "I have to wonder how many others there may be."

At the hearing, Melanson still denied all of his crimes, including the rapes in Texas and murders in Colorado and California. It was all a big misunderstanding, according to his statement to the board.

However, Young's letter to the board assured that there were no misunderstandings, and reminded them of the devastation he'd caused. "In 1974, he came across a woman in the Colorado mountains who out of kindness and what she perceived to be the right thing to do, due to the remoteness of the area, gave him a ride to town.

"Instead of thanking Ms. Wallace and going his own way, he took advantage of her, murdered her, took her car and belongings and used them to finance his way across country. He showed no regard for Ms. Wallace or her life. He saw her as an object and an opportunity. He denied her of the life, dreams and opportunities she had before her."

Although she was prohibited from talking about George Sr.'s murder, Young noted that Michele's death had torn the family apart and continued to haunt them. "Melanson chose to conceal Ms. Wallace's remains in a remote area of the Colorado mountains in the hopes she would never be found. This act in itself added an additional agony to her family member's and friends' lives. In the 'not knowing' where Ms. Wallace was for nearly 20 years, they were unable to move forward, they were stuck, unable even to attempt to begin any sort of healing or recovery from their loss."

Young told the board that the family asked her to convey their plea that Melanson never be released from prison in Colorado. "They believe he is the true definition of evil and that he is a violent and dangerous predator who cannot be rehabilitated no matter his age. They believe he has and will continue to use his charm, guile and deception to take advantage of others for his own gain as he sees fit at any given time.

"Melanson's record speaks for itself. Whenever he is free from incarceration he commits evil; he harms and kills people, and he destroys the lives of his victims and the people connected to them. He has claimed no responsibility for his actions and has shown no remorse. He should never be released from prison."

Young says she has mixed emotions about the case. "I have no regrets about working the case, meeting George, being able to lay Michele to rest next to her mother, etcetera," she wrote for this update when asked what she thinks about when the topic of Michele Wallace or Roy Melanson comes up. "But at times it feels like a ghost from Christmas past that keeps creeping back into my life or defines me when it's not all I am about."

ACKNOWLEDGEMENTS

On the pages that preceded readers were exposed to horrific acts of violence committed by a thoroughly evil man and the equally heroic efforts of law enforcement it took to stop him and bring him to justice. But this book is also intended to portray what this sort of despicable individual can do to the lives of so many other people beyond those he brutally raped and murdered—the families, the friends, those who dedicated themselves to catching him, the communities that many years later are haunted by his acts, and even the journalists who wrote about his violence and its repercussions over the years. To the extent that the brutality of men like Roy Melanson makes anyone feel less safe, we are all their victims.

The three murders that make up the core of this book began in 1974. However, the killer's reign of terror began even earlier than that with his first attempted rape in 1962 and wasn't resolved until 2011 (and indeed there are likely many other victims). That's fifty years of evil to account for. As such, in order to give a sense of the how this story unfolded and affected individuals and communities, I've included parts of reports from various publications written over the years, including the Napa Valley Register, the San Francisco Chronicle, and The Denver Post, my own 2002 book NO STONE UNTURNED: The True Story of the World's Premier Forensic Investigators, and the findagrave.com website, as well as various court documents and interviews. I've attempted to give credit where credit is due through *footnotes and attribution, and if I've missed any then I hope they'll forgive the oversight.*

Additionally, readers of NO STONE UNTURNED will recognize the Michele Wallace homicide case from a section of that book. Fourteen years later, in spite of the repetition I hope SMOOTH TALKER filled in some of the gaps from the Wallace murder, as well as put it into context with the murders of Anita Andrews and Charlotte Sauerwin, and how resolving the three cases became interrelated.

There are many people to thank for their help and support in writing this book. I'll start with the professionals such as my friend Kathy Young Ireland, and my other friends and colleagues at NecroSearch International. I am also deeply indebted to Don Winegar, Paul Gero, and Leslie Severe, and Stanley Carpenter. This book became an Epic Mysteries episode on the Investigation Discovery channel and I'd like to thank those associated with that Sharlene Martin, Nancy Glass, Matthew Watts, Eric Neuhaus, Rocki Alt, and Lauren Saft. I'd also like to thank my friend, Donna Campeglia, and tell her how sorry I am for her loss of "Mush."

The editing in this book was greatly assisted by Ian Dickerson, Lorie Matteson, Kim Ristoff and Jacqueline Burch. And a deep thanks to Professor Cindy Whitney at Western State University in Gunnison for dropping everything (including beer) to secure photographs for me and the ID people.

I would be remiss not to thank my friend and partner at WildBlue Press, Michael Cordova, for putting up with my insanity, as well as the rest of the crew at WildBlue, Ashley Butler, Mackenzie Jackson, Carla Torrisi Jackson, Lauri Ver Schure, and Elijah Toten.

Most of all I want to thank you, the readers, without whom there'd be no reason to write these books. I'm YOUR fan.—Steve Jackson

Use this link to sign up for advance notice
of Steve Jackson's Next Book:
http://wildbluepress.com/AdvanceNotice

Word-of-mouth is critical to an author's long-term success.
If you appreciated this book please leave a review on the
Amazon sales page:
http://wbp.bz/smoothtalkerreviews

STEVE JACKSON

<u>Other WildBlue Press Books By Steve Jackson</u>

Bogeyman: *He Was Every Parent's Nightmare*
http://wbp.bz/bogeyman

No Stone Unturned: *The True Story of the World's Premier Forensic Investigators*
http://wbp.bz/nsu

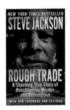

Rough Trade: *A Shocking True Story of Prostitution, Murder and Redemption*
http://wbp.bz/rt

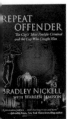

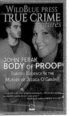

Let Someone Else Do The Reading.
Enjoy One Of Our Audiobooks

Learn more at: http://wbp.bz/audio